The Olden Time Series - Volume IV

HENRY MASON BROOKS

1886

TABLE OF CONTENTS

QUAINT AND CURIOUS ADVERTISEMENTS

QUAINT AND CURIOUS ADVERTISEMENTS

Among the mass of advertisements that have appeared from time to time in newspapers are to be found some which are very quaint and curious. Such are not, in all cases, intended by the writers to be so; but they sound so, especially to those persons who have an ear for strange or humorous things. Sometimes, indeed, it is the intention of the writers to attract particular notice by the wording of the advertisement. Oftentimes the matter may have been dictated by illiterate persons. Frequently the nature of the subject is itself sufficient to excite our humorous feelings. But whatever may be the object of the advertiser, these productions are often amusing and interesting enough to be reproduced for the benefit of those who cannot conveniently read the originals.

In 1767 "the Prince of the Power of the Air reigned with almost uncontrouled Restraint," according to a book published.

THIS DAY PUBLISHED,

An ADDRESS to

Persons of FASHION,

Concerning frequenting of

Plays, Balls, Assemblies, Card-Tables, andc.

In which is introduced the Character of

LUCINDA.

Printed and Sold by W. McAlpine, in Marlboro'-street.

*** A Pamphlet worthy the serious Attention of every Christian, especially at a Time when Vice and Immorality seems to have an Ascendency over Religion, and the Prince of the Power of the Air reigns with almost an uncontrouled Restraint.

(andirons), etc.

Sundry Things missing after the

late Fire, viz. One Pair of Brass Doggs, cast solid, very heavy and large; 22 yards of Hamburgh Sheeting; one Bell metal Skillet, and one Silver Spoon—The Persons that took them in not knowing who they may belong to, I take this Method to inform them that they belong to the Subscriber.

Jonathan Payson.

Lead sashes in use in 1767.

TO BE SOLD,

A Number of Windows, set in

Lead. Inquire of the Printers.

BOSTON, Printed by Edes and Gill, 1767.

In July, 1761, among the rough element, there seems to have been a "boom" in breaking windows and throwing stones. This state of things reached such a pitch that the Governor was forced to issue a Proclamation offering a reward for the detection of the offenders.

By His Excellency

Francis Bernard, Esq;

Captain-General and Governor in Chief, in and over His Majesty's Province of the Massachusetts Bay, in New-England, and Vice-Admiral of the same.

A PROCLAMATION.

Whereas certain Persons, who remain hitherto undiscovered, have of late committed great Disorders in the Night-Time, within several Towns in this Province, and particularly have broke the Windows of some Meeting Houses, and of the Dwelling-Houses of several Persons, by flinging thereinto great Stones and Bricks, thereby indangering the Lives of the Inhabitants, as well as injuring their Houses, against the Peace of our Sovereign Lord the King, and in Contempt of his Laws:

I have therefore thought fit, with the Advice of His Majesty's Council, to issue this Proclamation, requiring all Justices of the Peace, Sheriffs, Constables, and all other Officers whom it may concern, and also recommending it to all other His Majesty's good Subjects within this Province, to use their utmost Endeavours for discovering and bringing to Justice all Persons concerned in such disorderly and riotous Practices.

And I do hereby promise, that whosoever shall discover and detect all or any of the Persons concerned therein, so that they or any of them may be lawfully convicted of any such Offences, shall receive out of the Public Treasury of this Province the Sum of TEN POUNDS Lawful Money, as a Reward to be paid upon the Conviction of such Offender or Offenders.

GIVEN at the Council-Chamber in Boston, the Seventh Day of July, 1761, in the First Year of the Reign of our Sovereign Lord GEORGE the Third, by the Grace of GOD, of Great-Britain, France, and Ireland, KING, Defender of the Faith, andc.

Fr. Bernard.

By His Excellency's Command,

A. Oliver, Secr.

GOD Save the KING.

In the "Boston Gazette," this same year, August 10, Samuel Smith objected to people reporting that he "was run away."

WHEREAS it has been falsely reported by some ill minded litigious Persons that I, the Subscriber, was run away, THIS is to inform the Public, and especially those that it doth concern, That I have been no further than Philadelphia, a Trading, with a Design to return Home in about two Months, but return'd Home one Week sooner; and be it KNOWN notwithstanding all the false Reports about me, I am to be spoke with at my Dwelling-House at the North End, or upon 'Change, every Day in the Week.

Samuel Smith.

N.B. Said Smith has a House at the North End of the Town to Lett; also two Rooms in another House in said Part of the Town; he has likewise another House in said Part of the Town, which he would be willing to exchange for one further Southward.

Quaint advertisement of a paper-maker in the "Boston Gazette," Nov. 23, 1767.

ADVERTISEMENTS.

The Manufacturers of PAPER at

Milton beg the Favor of the Public to furnish them with what Linnen Rags they can spare, for which the greatest possible Allowance will be given.— All Persons dispos'd in this Way to encourage so useful a Manufacture, are hereby acquainted that Linnen Rags and old Paper (to be kept separate from each other) will be receiv'd at the following Places, viz.

In Boston, at Mr. Caleb Davis's Shop near the Fortification, Mr. Thomas Chase near Liberty-Tree, Mr. Andrew Gillespie, Tobacconist, in Fore-Street, Mr. John Bois's House in Long-Lane, and at Edes and Gill's Printing-Office in Queen-Street.——At Mr. Ellson's Master of the Workhouse in Salem; at Mr. Williams's Master of the Workhouse in Marblehead, to each of whom we have been already much oblig'd.——At Mr. Bulkeley Emerson Stationer in Newbury-Port, and at Mr. Daniel Fowle's, Printer in Portsmouth.——If any Person will favor us in this Way, who live near Winnisimet-Ferry, or in Black Horse Lane in Boston, or in the Center of the Town of Charlestown, they are desir'd to send their Names to Edes and Gill's Printing-Office.——As large Quantities of Paper fortunately arriv'd from Europe before the Duties could be demanded, it is hoped before that can be consum'd, there will be sufficient of this Country Manufacture for future Use.

The Printers of this Paper beg Leave to Advertise their Customers, that they have lately purchas'd a new Set of Types, at a very great Expence, which will be improved for the Entertainment and Instruction of the Public. They only desire that those Gentlemen who are in Arrears for more than a Twelvemonth, wou'd be kind enough for their Encouragement to pay off their respective Balances, as soon as may be, in Cash, or good clean Linnen Rags, the latter of which they prefer.

*** Choice WRITING PAPER, manufactured at Milton, to be Sold by the Printers hereof.

As Mr. Turner, the dancing-master, had "suffered much by booking," we infer that some people had "danced without paying the fiddler."

DANCING ACADEMY,

CONCERT-HALL.

Mr. Turner informs the Ladies

and Gentlemen in town and country, that he has reduced his price for teaching, from Six Dollars entrance to One Guinea, and from Four Dollars per month to Three. Those Ladies and Gentlemen who propose sending their children to be taught, will notice, that no books will be kept, as Mr. T. has suffered much by booking. The pupils must pay monthly, if they are desirous the School should continue.

Boston, March 29, 1788.

Mary Billings, opposite the Governor's, sold lottery tickets in 1761. (December 7.)

A Few TICKETS in

SUDBURY — LOTTERY,

Which will certainly commence Drawing on the 22d of this Month, may be had of the Managers in Sudbury or of Edes and Gill and Green and Russell, Printers in Queen-Street Boston.

SCHEME

1 of 500 Dollars. 180 of 10 Dollars.

15 of 100 80 of 8

20 of 50 51 of 6

20 of 40 1315 of 4

10 of 20

To be Sold by Mary Billings, opposite the Governor's—Cardinal Silks and Trimmings, with many other Articles, cheap for Cash.

From "Boston Gazette," Sept. 8, 1760:

To be Sold by Henry Paget, of Providence, a Tract of Land, partly improved, lying in Weyer River Parish, being the North Part of said Parish, and joins to Greenwich and Hardwick, containing about 2400 Acres—laid out in 100 Acre Lotts; to be Sold together, or in Lots. Said Land will be Sold reasonable for prompt Pay; or if the Purchaser can't pay the whole, good Security will be taken.

N.B. There's a settled Minister in said Parish much approved of.

Sporting in Boston, in 1790. From the "Massachusetts Centinel," May 1.

Whereas great danger daily arises to the Inhabitants, from the frequency of persons gunning or shooting birds, at various parts of the town, in direct violation of the law; the Selectmen would now acquaint the inhabitants, that they have appointed Mr. SHUBAEL HEWES to take notice of all such persons, who may be found shooting within the limits of the town in future, and prosecute them, without exception, to the utmost extent of the law.

PAUL REVERE AS A DENTIST.

In the "Boston Gazette," Dec. 19, 1768, appears the following curious advertisement:

Whereas many Persons are so

unfortunate as to lose their Fore-Teeth by Accident, and otherways, to their great Detriment, not only in Looks, but speaking both in Public and Private:—This is to inform all such, that they may have them re-placed with artificial Ones, that looks as well as the Natural, and answers the End of Speaking to all Intents, by PAUL REVERE, Goldsmith, near the Head of Dr. Clarke's Wharf, Boston.

*** All Persons who have had false Teeth fixt by Mr. John Baker, Surgeon-Dentist, and they have got loose (as they will in Time) may have them fastened by the above, who learnt the Method of fixing them from Mr. Baker.

Escape of a negro man slave who "can play on a Fiddle, and loves strong Drink."

FIVE DOLLARS Reward.

Ran-away from his Master the 25th Day of November last, at North-Kingston, in the Colony of Rhode-Island, a well-set Negro Man Slave, named Isaac, about 5 Feet 6 or 7 Inches high, with a Scar on his Forehead, between 30 and 40 Years old, thick Beard, can play on a Fiddle, and loves strong Drink; had on and carried with him a lightish-colour'd Thick-set Coat, a blue Ratteen Jacket with Cuffs to the Sleeves, a blue Broad Cloth Jacket without Sleeves, Flannel Shirt, stript Flannel Trowsers, grey yarn Stockings, and single Channel Pumps. Whoever will secure said Slave in any of his Majesty's Goals, or deliver him to the Subscriber, his Master, shall have FIVE DOLLARS Reward, and necessary Charges paid.

Per SAMUEL ROSE.

Masters of Vessels, and others, are hereby forbid carrying off or securing said Slave, as they would avoid the Penalty of the Law.

December 5, 1768.

Boston Gazette.

The town of Beverly has always been noted for beans, and it will be seen that as early as 1771 Josiah Woodbury offered two bushels as a reward to any person who would keep his "House Plague," who had run away from

him. The question naturally arises, Was "Old Moll" Mr. Woodbury's wife?
Beverly, Sept. 16, 1771.

Ran-away from Josiah Woodbury, Cooper, his House Plague for 7 long Years, Masury Old Moll, alias Trial of Vengeance. He that lost will never seek her; he that shall keep her, I will give two Bushel of Beans. I forewarn all Persons in Town or Country from trusting said Trial of Vengeance. I have hove all the old Shoes I can find for Joy; and all my Neighbours rejoice with me. A good Riddance of bad Ware. Amen.

Josiah Woodbury.

Essex Gazette, Sept. 17, 1771.

A woman advertises and describes a run-away husband.

Curious ADVERTISEMENT.

Copied from a late Hartford Paper.

Ran away from the subscriber, on the 13th of May, one Joseph Randall, a tall, trim-built fellow: Had on, when he went away, a blue coat, velvet waistcoat and breeches, mixt coloured stockings, and wore away two felt hats; he rode away a black horse, and led a sorrel horse; he is supposed to be lurking in the south part of Scantick after a strumpet that he has spent the most of his time with for three years past. Whoever will take up said Randall, and return him to me, shall have 3 coppers reward; but whoever will take the trouble to keep him away shall have ten dollars reward, and all necessary charges paid by me.

Susannah Randall.

N.B. All persons are forbid harbouring him, for I am determined to maintain him no longer.

Salem Mercury, July 1, 1785.

In the "Massachusetts Gazette," Feb. 3, 1774, is advertised a book by the notorious Dr. Dodd, who was executed for the forgery of Lord Chesterfield's name. This book is said to be "extremely proper to be given at Funerals."

A Book which upon perusal

recommends itself, and which it is only necessary to read to approve; extremely proper to be given at Funerals or any other solemn Occasion: being written expressly with that intention.

THIS DAY WAS PUBLISHED,

(Price 2s. Lawful Money single and 1/8. the doz.)

By Thomas Leverett, Nicholas Bowes

and Henry Knox in Cornhill,

REFLECTIONS

ON

DEATH.

By WILLIAM DODD, LL. D.

Prebendary of Brecon and Chaplain in Ordinary

to His Majesty.

It is appointed once for men to die, but
after this the Judgment, Heb. ix. 27.

THE FIFTH EDITION.

A desire of extending the very laudable Practice of giving Books at Funerals, and the great propriety of the present Work for that Purpose, have induced the Editors to put this valuable Performance one Third cheaper than the London Edition, although it is by no Means Inferior in point of Elegance.

Some of the business localities of Boston in the last century were known by names which now strike us as very queer or quaint. We select a number of advertisements from the "Gazette," "Post-Boy," and "Chronicle."

Dec. 10, 1759.

Imported in the last Ships from LONDON.

By Andrew Craigie,

And to be Sold at his Shop, right against the Old South Meeting-House: by Wholesale and Retail,

English Goods, suitable for the Season, too many to be enumerated, At the lowest Rate, for Cash, or short Credit.

Feb. 23, 1761.

Isaac Dupee, Carver,

Advertises his Customers and others that since the late Fire (on Dock Square) he has opened a Shop the North Side of the Swing-Bridge, opposite to Thomas Tyler's, Esq.; where Business will be carried on as usual with Fidelity and Dispatch.

Imported in the Neptune, Capt. Binney, and to be Sold by

Daniel Parker, Goldsmith,

At his Shop near the Golden-Ball, Boston.

An Assortment of Articles in the Goldsmith's and Jeweller's Way, viz. brilliant and cypher'd Button and Earing Stones of all Sorts, Locket Stones, cypher'd Ring Stones, Brilliant Ring Sparks, Buckle Stones, Garnetts, Emethysts, Topaz and Saphire Ring Stones, neat Stone Rings sett in Gold, some with Diamond Sparks, Stone Buttons in Silver, by the Card, black ditto in Silver, best Sword Blades, Shoe and Knee Chapes of all Sizes, Files of all Sorts, freezing Punches, Turkey Oyl Stones, red and white Foyl, moulding Sand, Borax, Saltpetre, Crucibles and Black Led Potts, Money Scales, large ditto to weigh Silver, Piles of Ounce Weights, Penny Weights and Grains, Coral Beeds, Stick ditto for Whistles, Forgeing Anvils, Spoon Teats, plain ditto, small raizing Anvils for Cream Potts, fine Lancashire Watch Plyers, Shears and Nippers, Birmingham ditto, with sundry other Articles, cheap for Cash.

Choice Muscovado best Powder and brown Sugars, by the Hogshead or Barrel, to be Sold by WILLIAM WHITWELL, at the Seven Stars near the

Draw-Bridge, Boston. Also choice new Raisins by the Cask, Philadelphia Flour and Bar Iron per Quantity, Coffee by the Barrel or Hundred, Bohea Tea, andc., cheap for Cash or short Credit.

Sept. 8, 1760.

John Loring,

At his Shop near The Great Trees.

A Fresh and General Assortment of Medecines both Chemical and Galenical—Spices of all Sorts—Likewise Redwood, Logwood, Allum, Copperas, Brimstone, andc.——N.B. True Lockyer's Pills, Bateman's Drops, Stoughton's and Duffy's Elixer, andc. andc.

Susannah Foster

Hereby informs her Customers, That she has removed from Queen Street to Fore-Street, next Door to the Sign of the Cross, where they may be supplied as usual with all Kinds of Groceries at the cheapest Rates.

Feb. 23, 1761.

Imported in the last Ship from London, and to be Sold

By Thomas Allen.

Near Bromfield's Lane, BOSTON.

Cardinal Silks and Trimmings, Prussian Cloaks, Muffs and Tippets, Callimanco and Tammy quilted Coats, Irish Linens, Mens and Womens cotton, thread and worsted Hose; a neat Assortment of Millenary Goods, andc. cheap for Cash.—

ALSO a great Variety of Paper Hangings.

Imported in Captains Hulme and Binney from London,

By Thomas Handasyd Peck,

And Sold by him at the Hatt and Beaver, Merchant's Row.

A Fresh Assortment of Linnen Linings, suitable for Beaver, Beaverett, Castor and Felt Hatts, Tabby ditto, Mohair Lupings, Silk Braid ditto, flatt and round Silk Lace and Frogs for Button Lupes, plain and sash Bands, workt and plain Buttons, black Thread, Gold and Silver Chain, yellow and white Buttons, hard and light Brushes, Velures, Cards, large and small Bowstrings, Looping Needles, Verdigrees and Coperas, a good Assortment of Mens and Boys Felt Hatts, Castor ditto.——He likewise sells Logwood.

Missing since the late Fire, when the Market-House was burnt, a large Folio of Mr. Clarkson's Works, and twenty yards of Gold and Silver Chain. If any Person has the Book or Chain, they are desir'd to inform said Peck.

May 11, 1761.

A few Firkins of Choice Butter,

to be Sold by PHILIP FREEMAN, at the Blue Glove, facing the Sign of the Cornfields.

May 11, 1761.

Jonathan and John Amory

In King-Street, just below the Town-House in Boston, and at Salem, in the

House where the Honourable Timothy Lindal, Esq; deceas'd, lately dwelt, near the Friends Meeting House, Have lately open'd a very large Assortment of English Goods, of almost every Kind, for Men's and Women's wear, consisting of too many Articles to be compriz'd in an Advertisement, which they will sell at either Place, by Wholesale or Retail, at very low Prices for Cash or Treasurer's Notes, and allow the Interest thereon.

May 11, 1761.

Imported by

John and Thomas Stevenson,

And to be Sold at their Shop, at the Sign of the Stays, opposite the South Side of the Town-House, Boston, at the very lowest Prices, Viz.

Lawns of all Sorts, strip'd

and flower'd kenting Handkerchiefs; cotton and linnen ditto; silk and gause ditto; Cambricks, Calicoes and printed Linnens—white and colour'd Threads;—silk, worsted, cotton and thread Stockings—Women's silk and worsted Mitts—Broad-Cloths; German Serges—Thicksets; Fustians; Jeans; Pillows and Dimities—Broglios; Dorsateens; Venetian Poplins; flower'd and plain Damasks; Prussianets; Serpentines; Tammies; strip'd Stuffs; Camblets; Callimancoes; Shalloons and Buckrams,—worsted Caps; Garters; Needles and Pins—white, brown and striped Hollands—white and check'd Linnen; Diaper; Bed-Ticks; Tartans; Plaids; Breeches and Jacket Stocking Patterns; cotton and silk and cotton Gowns—Stock Tapes—Leather Breeches; Men's and Women's Leather Shoes, andc. andc.

N.B. Kippen's and Tilloch's Snuff; Scotch Barley and Carpeting and Porter by the Dozen; With a great Number of other Articles.

Jan. 9, 1764.

A Few Hogsheads of choice

Barbadoes RUM to be sold: Inquire Nathaniel Abraham, at the Golden Key.

TO BE LETT,

And enter'd upon the 25th of March, in good

tenable Repair.

The Five Grist-Mills at the North Part of the Town of Boston, with Stabling for Horses, Stores for Grain, andc. Any Person inclining to Hire, may apply to William Hunt, in Hanover-Street, whom the Proprietors hath empowered to Let the same.

Feb. 23, 1767.

May 4, 1767.

Just Imported from London, and to be Sold by

Daniel Boyer, Jeweller,

At his Shop opposite the Governor's in Boston,

Best Brilliant and   *   Binding Wire

Cypher Earing and Button * Brass and Iron ditto
Stones * Brass stamps
Brilliant and cypher ring * Buckle and ring brushes
stones * Money scales and weights
Garnets, amethysts, and * Small sheers and plyers
topaz * Screw dividers
Ring and buckle sparks * Blow pipes
Locket stones and cyphers * Draw plates
Ruby and white foyle * Moulding sand
Coral beeds * Crucibles and black pots
Coral for whistles * Borax and Salt-Petre
Shoe and knee chapes * Pommice and Rottenstone,
Rough and smooth files * andc.
Where also may be had, most sorts of Jewellers
and Goldsmith Work, cheap for Cash.
William Palfrey
Hereby informs his Customers and others, That he has just opened a fresh
Assortment of Goods suitable for the Season, which were imported in the
Ship Boston-Packet, Capt. Marshall.
ALSO, A Variety of Stone, China and Glass Ware, which will be sold very
low at his Shop next Door North of the Heart and Crown in Cornhill,
Boston.
Imported in Captain Skillings from London, and to
be Sold
By John Symmes, Goldsmith,
Near the Golden Ball, Boston, viz.
Best Shoe and Knee Buckles Fluke and Tongs, ruff and smooth Files, Bone
Buckle Brushes, Freezing Punches, Binding Wire, Steel Top Thimbles,
Cypher and Brilliant Button Stones, Cypher and Brilliant Ring Stones, Ring
Sparks, Motto Ring Stones, Amethysts, Garnetts, Brilliant and Cypher
Earing Stones, Amethysts Foyle, red and white do. Stone Bosom Buckles,
Crusables, and Black Lead Melting Pots, andc. all cheap for Cash.
November, 1767.
Robert Duncan
Begs Leave to inform his Customers and Others, That he has removed
from the Store on the Town Dock to the Shop lately improved by Mr.
William Palfrey, next Door Northward of the Sign of the HEART and
CROWN in Cornhill.
A House to Lett in Hawkins's-Street, near the Sign of the Parrot. Inquire of
Edes and Gill.
No. 1. A House at the North-End of the Town, the Corner of Winnisimett
Ferry.
No. 4. One large double House at New-Boston, near the Sign of the Ship.

Boston, 21st Nov. 1767.

Aug. 13, 1759.

Imported in the last Ships from London, and to be Sold

By John Townley,

At the Sign of the Wheat Sheaff, the Corner of Wing's Lane, very cheap for Cash;

Broad cloths, Yorkshire plains, cotton velvets and cut-velvet shapes, thicksetts, fustians, white jeans, figured and corded dimothys, silk and cotton gowns, stript linnens, Manchester checks, ruffells, calimancoes, tammys, durants, yard wide and prussian poplins, cross-bar'd stuffs, rich brunets, broglios, stript and plain camblets and cambleteens, lastings of all colours, bombazine, a fine assortment of Irish linnens, English oznabrigs.

Imported in the last Ships from LONDON, by

Ebenezer Coffin,

And to be Sold at the Crown and Bee-Hive, opposite Deacon Phillips's in Cornhill, Boston, very cheap for ready Cash, or on short Credit,

A Large assortment of best london, hard-metal and common pewter dishes, plates, basons, porringers, quart-pots, tankards, soup-kettles, communion flaggons and cups, christening basons, tea-pots and spoons, bed and close stool pans, measures, andc.

Aug. 27, 1759.

Adino Paddock Chaise-Maker,

near the Granary, has six second-hand Chaises to sell; and as they take up much Storage, he will sell them under their Value.

Aug. 22, 1763.

Benjamin Russell

Informs his Customers and others, that he Undertakes PAPERING ROOMS and Stair-Cases in the best Manner, at a reasonable Rate.—Any Gentleman that has a mind to Employ him in the neighbouring Towns, may be serv'd by him (paying his Travelling Charges) at the same Rate as those in Boston.—Said Russell has a number of Window SASHES 10 by 8, 24 Lights in a Window, to Sell reasonably for Cash,—they are made of the best of Pine.

☞ Said Russell lives the North-side of Bacon-Hill in Boston, opposite to Mr. Joseph Callender's, Baker.

Jan. 12, 1767.

TO BE SOLD BY

Joseph Palmer and Co.,

At their Store on Minot's T,

Spermaceti Candles, warranted Pure—Spermaceti in Cakes—Strain'd Spermaceti Oyl, by the Quantity or Cask—Philadelphia Flour—English Duck, Cordage, andc.

A few Firkins of choice good Irish

BUTTER, to be Sold by BLANCHARD and HANCOCK, opposite the Conduit.——Likewise a large and good assortment of Ironmongery, Cutlery and Pewter Wares, just imported in the Lydia, Captain Scott, from London—Also, Philadelphia and Russia Barr Iron, andc. all at the very lowest Rates for Cash.

June 14, 1762.

Good cyder to be Sold by

the Barrel, or otherwise, at the Black Boy and But, by JONATHAN WILLIAMS.

Daniel Jones,

At the HAT and HELMIT, South-End, Boston,

Makes Beaver and Beaveret

HATS; has also English Beaveret and Castor, English and French Felt Hats, Hat Trimmings; an Assortment of English GOODS suitable for all Seasons of the Year; a few Boxes of Looking-Glasses; which he will sell by Wholesale or Retail at a moderate Rate for Cash, Treasurer's Notes, or short Credit.

N.B. Said Jones desires those Persons who have far exceeded their Contracts either on Book or Notes of Hand, to be very speedy in settling the same, or they will oblige him to the disagreeable Necessity of putting them to Trouble.

All Persons that are indebted

to the Estate of James Mason, late of Boston, Merchant, Deceas'd, are desired to Pay the same without Delay to Jonathan Mason, Executor to his Will;—and those who have any Demands on said Estate, are desired to bring in their Accompts to said Executor, who has to Sell at his House next Door to the Sign of the Three Kings in Cornhill, the following GOODS belonging to the Estate of the Deceased, which will be Sold at the first Cost and Charges, Viz.

Broad Cloths, German Serges,

Bearskins, Beaver Coating, Half-Thick, red Shagg, Bayes, 8 qr. and 9 qr. Blankets, Shalloons, Tammies, Durants, Calimancoes, worsted Damasks, strip'd and plain Camblets, strip'd Swanskins, Flannell, Manchester Velvet, Womens ditto, Bombazeen, Allopeen, colour'd Ruffells, Hungarians, Dimothy, Crimson and green China, 7-8th, yard wide and 6 qr. cotton Check, worsted and Hair Plush, Men's and Women's Hose, worsted Caps, mill'd ditto, black Tiffany, Women's and Children's Stays, cotton Romalls, printed Linnen Handkerchiefs, black Gauze ditto, Bandanoes, Silk Lungee Romalls, Cambricks, Lawns, Muslins, Callicoes, Chints, Buckrams, Gulick Irish and Tandem Holland, Mens and Womens Kid and Lamb Gloves, black and white Bone Lace, Capuchin Silk, and Fringe, Gartering, Silk and Cotton Laces, stript Gingham, yellow Canvas, Diaper, Damask Table Cloths and Napkins, Bedtick, 7-8th Garlix, Soletare Necklaces and Earings,

Tapes, Womens Russel Shoes, sewing Silk, Nutmegs, Pepper, Looking Glasses, Ticklinburg, English and Russia Duck, Allum, Copperas and Brimstone, German Steel, Bar Lead, English and India Taffety, Grograms, English and India Damasks, Padusoys, Lutestrings, black and white Sattin, rich Brocade, Gauze Caps, and Ruffles, Shades and handsome Silk Cloaks, and.c. andc. andc.

Aug. 22, 1763.

Andrew Barclay,

At his House opposite the Golden Cock in Marlborough-Street, Boston, Binds Books of all kinds, Gilt and Plain, in the neatest and best Manner. Gentlemen in Town or Country may depend upon having their Work done with Fidelity and Dispatch.

1768. Nov. 21.———Nov. 28.

Just imported in the Ship Thames, Captain Watt, from London, by

Samuel Franklin,

At the Sign of the Crown and Razor, South-End, Boston:

Best Razors, Pen-knives, scissars,

shears, shoe-knives, shoe tacks and stampt awl blades, teeth instruments, lancets, white and yellow swords, and sword belts; case-knives and forks; ink powder and sealing-wax, files and rasps; horse sleams; hones and curling tongs; brass ink-pots, horn and ivory combs; white, yellow and steel shoe and knee buckles; gilt, lackered and plated coat and breast buttons, snuff boxes, and a few second hand hats, andc. all very cheap.

N.B. Razors, penknives and scissars ground, scabbards made for swords and bayonets, caseknife and fork blades made at said Shop.

Boston Chronicle.

1769. June 1.———June 5.

WINE

TO BE SOLD by

ROSANNA MOORE,

By wholesale and retail, at her WINE CELLAR

near LIBERTY TREE, Boston, viz.

Old Sterling Madeira, Lisbon,

Teneriff, Claret, Port, Canary, Malaga, Tent, sweet and other WINES, all in their original purity, and as cheap as any in town.

Boston Chronicle, June 1, 1769.

Just imported from LONDON, by

Jolley Allen,

At his Shop about Midway between the Governor's and the Town-House, and almost Opposite the Heart and Crown in Cornhill,

BOSTON.

A very large Assortment of English and India GOODS, fit for all Seasons, too many to be enumerated separately in an Advertisement.———

Boston Gazette, Feb. 20, 1767.

WHEREAS the CO-PARTNERSHIP of

Chase and Speakman is mutually

dissolved, this is to desire all persons who are indebted to them to make speedy payment, and likewise all those who have any demands on said company, to call and receive their respective dues of T. Chase, at the venerable LIBERTY-ELM.

Boston Chronicle, May 22, 1769

BOSTON.

This morning arrived here Captain Paddock, in a schooner from London, after a long passage.

***The BOSTONIAN came too late for this day's Paper.

STOLEN,

From the side of the house, belonging to Richard Silvester, now the Sign of the

BROKEN POST,

Newbury street, Boston, about half an hour past one o'clock in the morning of the 24th ult.

A Black and White Horse, with

a Bridle, without a Saddle.——The Persons concerned in this Frolick, who were seen and known, are desired to replace the said Horse, in the manner and form they found him. And it is hoped, as he is a young creature, they will not corrupt his morals, by teaching him any of their bad tricks, but return him soon, as the owner will not allow any thing for his keeping.

N.B. If he should bite or kick any that have him in possession; his former master now declares, he will not be answerable for the damages.——He was not imported from England, but manufactured in this land of liberty.

Query. Whether the persons who knocked at said Silvester's door, past three o'clock the same morning, in their return home, and cried Thieves, were not accomplices in this glorious exploit.

Boston Chronicle, March 1, 1770.

TO BE SOLD

By Mary Jackson and Son,

At the Brazen-Head

in Cornhill,

A few Firkins of good Butter, at

4s. 6d. per Pound; also choice Connecticut Pork, Hogs Fat, and Cheese.

N.B. All Kind of Braziers, Cutlers, Pewterers and Ironmongery Goods, Wholesale and Retail.

July 13, 1761.

WANTED for a HOUSE-KEEPER,

A Discreet elderly WOMAN that can be well recommended, who understands dressing victuals, and the œconomy of a large family where there are no children.—Such a person will meet with good encouragement, by applying to Mein and Fleeming.

Boston Chronicle, Dec. 19, 1768.

To be SOLD by

JOHN CROSBY,

LEMMON-TRADER, at the Sign of the Basket of LEMMONS, at the South-End, Choice good and fresh LISBON LEMMONS, equal to any in Town for goodness, and as large in general as Lemmons commonly are, at Four Pounds O.T. per Hundred, and Ten Shillings per single Dozen.

Dec. 19, 1768.

TO BE LET,

A Handsome square SHOP, in Marshall's-Lane, near Boston-stone, suitable either for a Grocery, West-India or Dry-Goods Shop—it will also accommodate any person in the Mechanical Line. Inquire of the Printer, or of GILES RICHARDS and Co. near the Mill-Bridge.

March 12, 1791.

Picture of a Boston mariner in 1799.

TO BE SOLD,

By Samuel Thaxter,

Mathematical

Instrument Maker,

No. 49 State-Street,

1 best brass Sextant, latest improvement; Hadley's Quadrants, Davis' do. Brass Azimuth Amplitude and Steering Compas; Brass Surveying Compas, Wood, do. Spy Glasses; Sea Books, and Charts; Scales and Dividers; Surveying Chains, andc.

n.b. Quadrants and Compasses carefully repaired;—where Gentlemen may depend on reasonableness and punctuality.

March 30.

FOR SALE,

A Small HOUSE-LOT, in Sisters-lane, very near the Rev. Dr. Belknap's Meeting-house. Inquire of the Printer.

March 30. 1799.

Just Imported, and to be Sold by

Harbottle Dorr,

At his Shop (adjoining to the House of Mr. Martin Gay) almost opposite to the Cornfields in Union-Street, Boston,

A Fine Assortment of Braziery, Ironmongery, and Cutlery Ware, by Wholesale or Retail, cheap for Cash.

Boston Gazette, July 13, 1767.

A sermon suitable to distribute among tenants and servants:—

THIS DAY PUBLISHED,

(And Sold by S. Kneeland, in Queen-Street;)

The CARE of the SOUL,
urged as the One Thing Needful. A SERMON first preached at the Funeral
of a young Person, and afterwards before some worthy and excellent
Persons, who desired some printed Copies of it, to disperse among their
Tenants and Servants.
Boston Gazette, Nov. 2, 1761.
Goods exchanged for New England rum.
Barbados Rum, Russia Duck
and Sugars by the Hogshead or Barrel, Pitch, Tar, and
Bohea Tea, Cordage.
Cotton Wool by the Bag, Long and short Pipes.
New Flour, Sole Leather.
Indigo. English Steel.

☞ Dumb FISH. With,
A General Assortment of English Goods and Hard Ware.
Many of the above Articles will be Exchang'd for New England Rum,
By Samuel Allyne Otis,
At Store No. 5, South-Side of the Town-Dock.
Boston Gazette, Sept. 22, 1767.
Wigs advertised in Salem, suitable to "grace and become Judges, Divines,
Lawyers, or Physicians," and "Rolls to raise the Heads" of ladies "to any
Pitch they desire." This shop was probably patronized by Judge and Madam
Lynde, Colonel Pickman, Dr. Holyoke, Dr. Barnard, Dr. Hopkins, Dr.
Whitaker, Samuel Curwen, Judge Ropes, John Appleton, Deacon Holman,
Friend Northey, and others.
William Lang,
Wig-Maker and Hair-Dresser,
Hereby informs the Public, that he has hired a Person from EUROPE, by
whose Assistance he is now enabled, in the several Branches of his
Business, to serve his good Customers, and all others, in the most genteel
and polite Tastes that are at present in Fashion in England and America.——
——In particular, WIGS made in any Mode whatever, such as may grace and
become the most important Heads, whether those of Judges, Divines,
Lawyers or Physicians; together with all those of an inferior Kind, so as
exactly to suit their respective Occupations and Inclinations.——HAIR-
DRESSING, for Ladies and Gentlemen, performed in the most elegant and
newest Taste.——Ladies, in a particular Manner, shall be attended to, in the
nice, easy, genteel and polite Construction of ROLLS, such as may tend to
raise their Heads to any Pitch they desire,——also French Curls, made in
the neatest Manner. He gives Cash for Hair.
Essex Gazette, Feb. 9, 1773.
On the departure of Governor Hutchinson from the Province of
Massachusetts in 1774, a hundred and twenty-three citizens of Boston,

together with sundry citizens of Salem, Marblehead, and other places, signed a complimentary address to him, "lamenting the loss of so good a Governor," and praising him for his character and conduct. Most of these persons belonged to the better classes; but their action was judged to be, to say the least, hasty. Shortly after this, these "addressors" were "hauled over the coals" by the patriots and forced to retract. The following cards from some of these gentlemen we take from the "Essex Gazette," a newspaper circulating in Salem and Cambridge. From the known character and standing of many of these persons, it is believed that they were glad of an opportunity of thus expressing their patriotism. The first blood of the Revolution had not been shed when they signed this address to the Governor, who they had hoped would be able to influence the British ministry so that war could be averted. But after the battles of Lexington and Concord there was no longer any hope of a reconciliation, and the "Committee of Safety," naturally wishing to be sure as to who were friends and who were enemies, took this method of ascertaining the fact and thereby satisfying the community.

Salem, May 30, 1775.

Whereas we the Subscribers did some time since sign an Address to Governor Hutchinson, which, though prompted to by the best Intentions, has nevertheless given great Offence to our Country; We do now declare that we were so far from designing by that Action to show our Acquiescence in those Acts of Parliament so universally and justly odious to all America, that on the contrary we hoped we might in that Way contribute to their Repeal, though now to our sorrow we find ourselves mistaken.— And we do now further declare that we never intended the Offense which this Address has occasioned, that if we had foreseen such an Event, we should never have signed it; as it always has been and now is our Wish to live in Harmony with our Neighbors, and our serious Determination to promote to the utmost of our Power, the Liberty, the Welfare and Happiness of our Country, which is inseparably connected with our own.

John Nutting, Andrew Dalgleish,
N. Goodale, Thomas Barnard,
E.A. Holyoke, Nath. Dabney,
Wm. Pynchon, William Pickman,
Eben'r Putnam, C. Gayton Pickman,
Francis Cabot, John Turner,
N. Sparhawk.

In Committee of Safety, Salem, 30th May, 1775.

The Declaration of which the above is a copy, being presented and read, it was voted unanimously that the same was satisfactory, and that the said Gentlemen ought to be received and treated as real Friends to this Country. By order of the Committee,

RICHARD DERBY, jun., Chairman.

Whereas I the Subscriber was so unfortunate (some Time since) as to sign an Address to the late Governor Hutchinson, so universally, and so justly, deemed an Enemy to American Liberty and Freedom, I hereby in this public Manner declare that at the Time I signed the said Address, I intended the Good of my Country, and that only; but finding in my Sorrow it had not that but quite a contrary Effect, I hereby renounce the same Address in every Part, and hope my injured and afflicted Fellow-Countrymen will overlook my past Misconduct, as I am ready to assist them in their Struggles for Liberty and Freedom in whatever Way I shall be called upon by them. Londonderry, June 6, 1775.

John Prentice.

To the Publick:

Whereas I the Subscriber signed an Address to the late Governor Hutchinson, upon his leaving this Province: I now declare my doing so was without any View of injuring the Liberties of my Country, which I ever held sacred; nor had I the least Design of giving Offence to any Individual within the Circle of my Acquaintance, and had I conceived such an Address would have been so generally disapproved of, I should by no Means have signed it; and hope the Publick will freely forgive this Error in their humble Servant.

Jonathan Glover.

Whereas I, the Subscriber, signed an Address to the late Governor Hutchinson,—I wish the Devil had had said Address before I had seen it. Marblehead, October 24, 1774.

J. Fowle.

John Prentice, of Marblehead, signed a similar card the same day.

We have room but for one more of these political cards. The Rev. Samuel Dana, of Groton, appears to have been suspected of "Toryism," and prints the following in the "Essex Gazette":—

"I, the Subscriber, being deeply affected with the Miseries bro't on this Country by a horrid Thirst for ill-got Wealth and unconstitutional Power,—and lamenting my Unhappiness in being left to adopt Principles in Politics different from the Generality of my Countrymen; and thence to conduct in a Manner that has but too justly excited the Jealousy and Resentment of the true Sons of Liberty against me, earnestly desirous, at the same Time, to give them all the Satisfaction in my Power; do hereby Sincerely ask Forgiveness of all such for whatever I have said or done, that had the least Tendency to the Injury of my Country, assuring them that it is my full Purpose, in my proper Sphere, to unite with them in all those laudable and fit Measures that have been recommended by the Continental and Provincial Congresses for the Salvation of this Country, hoping my future Conversation and Conduct will fully prove the up-rightness of my present

Professions.

Groton, May 22, 1775.

Samuel Dana.

The town of Groton voted that the above was satisfactory to the inhabitants, and that Mr. Dana "ought to enjoy the Privileges of Society," etc.

East Boston, to be let, in the year 1800.

Noddle's Island.

TO BE LET, (for the term of one or more years, and entered upon, the 25th March next,)

That valuable Estate in the Harbour of Boston, known by the name of Noddle's Island. The advantages of its situation, soil, andc. andc. are so well known, as to render a detail thereof unnecessary.—For particulars, inquire of the Printer, or of DAVID S. GREENOUGH, at Roxbury.

Feb. 15.

Columbian Centinel.

GENTLEMEN and LADIES.

Isaac Greenwood, jun., takes this opportunity to inform you, that at his Shop opposite the Town-House, in Salem, Gentlemen may be supplyed with neat walking Sticks; and Ladies with Umbrellas, neater and cheaper than those imported: He makes and mends Umbrella Sticks in the best Manner.

He earnestly wishes, for his Profit and their Good, that they would apply to him for Teeth-Brushes, and Teeth-Powder, which when used will recommend itself.

Said Greenwood performs all kinds of turned Work, in Silver, such as Tankards, Cans, andc. also in Brass, Iron, Ivory, Turtle-Shell, Bone, Horn, and Wood of any sort or bigness. Repairs Violins; makes Flutes, Fifes, Hoboys, Clarinets, Chaise-Whips, Tea-Boards, Bottle-Stands, Tamboy Frames, Back-Gammon Boxes Men and Dies, Chess men, Billiard-Balls, Maces, Lemon Squeezers, Serenges, Hydrometers, Shaving Boxes and Brushes, Buckle-Brushes, Ink-Stands, Paper-Folders, Sand-Boxes, Bannisters for Stair-Cases, andc. andc. andc.

Salem Gazette, July 3, 1781.

An appeal to "the Sentimentalists of the Town of Salem," from the "Gazette" of June 19, 1781. "Sentimentalists" would in these days be called book-buyers.

By AUTHORITY.

JEWELS and DIAMONDS for Sentimentalists.

The Sentimentalists of the Town of Salem, and all Voluntiers, who are pleased to encourage the extensive Propagation of polite Literature, by the Business of Book Auctioniering, which in all free States hath always been highly favoured with peculiar Privileges, because it is the sublimest Auxiliary which Science, Commerce, and Arts either has, or perhaps ever will possess, are requested to observe, that On Thursday Evening June 21st, 1781, and for two more Evenings successively, The following curious Collection of valuable and scarce BOOKS, containing History, Biography, Voyages, Travels, Philosophy, Mathematics, Periodical Papers, Letters, Essays, Arts, Sciences, Novels and Adventures, with Poetic and Dramatic Entertainment, by the most celebrated ancient and modern Authors, who have explored, investigated, and attempted to illuminate the human Understanding with the god-like Attribute of knowledge,

Will be exhibited by AUCTION, at Mr. Goodhue's Tavern in the Town of SALEM,

By ROBERT BELL, Bookseller, Provedore to the Sentimentalists, and Professor of Book-Auctioniering, who is just arrived from Philadelphia, and will return thither in a few days.

Hours of Exhibition by Auction from Six to Ten each Evening; when the Jewels and Diamonds will, instantaneously, either be sold or sacrificed, according to the Taste of the Company.

Printed CATALOGUES of the Books to be had at the Time and Place.

N.B. On Tuesday, or Wednesday next Week, the Book-Auctionier intends also to exhibit a Collection of Books by Auction in the town of Newbury-Port; and sometime in the Week after, he intends to exhibit another Collection of Books by Auction in the Town of Portsmouth, the Capital of the State of New-Hampshire.

In the "Herald of Freedom," published in Boston, is the following singular notice from Osgood Carleton:—

Osgood Carleton,

Having been frequently applied to for a decision of disputes, and sometimes wagers,[A] respecting the place of his nativity, and finding they sometimes operate to his disadvantage: Begs leave to give this public information—that he was born in Nottingham-west, in the State of New-Hampshire—in which state he resided until sixteen years old; after which time, he traveled by sea and land to various parts, and being (while young) mostly conversant with the English, he lost some of the country dialect, which gives rise to the above disputes.

[A] Several Englishmen have disputed his being born in America.

Boston, august 20, 1790.

The singular taste for wax-work exhibitions which used formerly to prevail is shown in the following announcement from the "Salem Gazette," Oct. 18, 1791:—

WAX-WORK.

Mr. BOWEN

Respectfully acquaints the Ladies and Gentlemen of Salem and its vicinity, that he has removed his Exhibition from Boston, where it met with universal applause.

To-Morrow Evening at 7 o'clock the door will be opened, and commence one of the most pleasing and innocent amusements,

At the Assembly Room, Salem.

The numerous attractions of this admired Collection having lately been increased by adding several excellent new Figures, it is recommended to be worthy of the patronage and attention of a liberal public. Mr. Bowen, wishing immediately to gratify the inhabitants of this town and vicinity, begs leave to inform them that his residence here will be but a few days.

It would be unnecessary to give a particular description of all the Figures in this large Exhibition; but among the most admired, we may enumerate, an excellent likeness of the President of the United States and his amiable Lady, with a representation of the President supporting the Union of Liberty, Justice, Peace, and Plenty. His Excellency Gov. Hancock, who was one of the first of the patriotic members that signed the Declaration of American Independence—a sincere Friend to his Country. The celebrated Hamilton, Secretary of the Treasury of the United States. Three beautiful female Figures, representing a Boston, Rhodeisland, and Philadelphia Beauty. The unfortunate Baron Trenck in real chains. Doctor Franklin, dressed in a suit of his own clothes, with about Twenty other Figures in full stature.

The Exhibition will be open every day (except Saturday evenings and Sundays) from 10 o'clock in the morning until 9 in the evening.

☞ Tickets of admission, at one shilling and six pence for Ladies and Gentlemen, and nine-pence for Children under 10 years of age, may be had at the door.

No reduction of the price will take place.

Wine advertised in a Baltimore paper in 1788.

"☞ In good Wine there is truth."

"The rosy God, ever attentive to the wants and wishes of his votaries here below, has for their use deposited in the hands of the subscriber (one of his oldest Tapsters) some of his CHOICEST GIFTS, the best Produce of various Vintages. Such exhilarating Beverage as, of old, cheered the Hearts of Gods and Men.—A strict Observance of the Seventh Commandment is enjoined in the Distribution. The Fiat shall be obeyed, by the Publick's most obliged and devoted Servant,

"THOMAS HEPBURN.

"Baltimore, April 11, 1788."

In the "Boston Columbian Centinel" Josiah Flagg, jun., advertises for "live teeth."

JOSIAH FLAGG, jun.

SURGEON DENTIST:

at the Stone-House, Beacon-Street,

BOSTON—

Continues his practise with useful improvements. Assistance to the poor gratis.

☞ CASH given for live Teeth, and Gold Cobbs, or Dust.

May 26, 1792.

It is curious to see how in "old times" things "got mixed up." The incongruity of putting together whalebone, Bibles, and chip hats is only exceeded by a later advertisement we have seen of Scott's Bible sold at a lottery-office. This is from the "Salem Mercury" of 1788:—

NEXT FRIDAY,

AT W.P. Bartlett's Office,

Will be Sold at

Publick Auction,

A variety of Shop Goods and

other articles:

Among which are,

A Few pieces best India BANDANNOES——BROADCLOTHS in patterns—twill'd and plain CORDUROY—few doz. purple and white SHAWLS—Hair Ribbons—coloured Threads—No 4 Pins—Irish LINENS—yellow SERGE—black LASTINGS—WHALEBONE—large and small BIBLES—Chip Hats—Watch Chains—Bottled Mustard— Playing Cards—Green Chairs—few pounds of NUTMEGS—Men's Worsted STOCKINGS, andc.—Sale to begin at 11 o'clock, a.m.

The following notice of the Bradford Academy from the "Salem Gazette" reminds us of the days of small prices,—"Tuition $3," or "$3.50 to those who paint and embroider"!

Bradford Academy.

The Female Apartment in Bradford Academy, half a mile from Haverhill Bridge, will be opened the first Wednesday in May, under the direction of approved instructors. The Male Apartment will be continued as usual. Young Masters and Misses will be instructed by such as are assigned to their respective Apartments, in all the branches hitherto taught in that or in any other Academy. The preceptor will spend less time than usual in the female apartment, and the preceptress will have an assistant. The price of tuition, except those who paint and embroider, will be three dollars a quarter. To those who paint and embroider, three dollars and fifty cents. Very particular attention will be paid to inculcate virtuous sentiments and preserve the moral character of the scholars.

Bradford, April 9, 1805.

Husbands often advertise wives, but it is seldom that a wife publicly refuses to pay her husband's debts, as according to the following announcement from the "Salem Gazette," Mistress Sarah Brooks did. This was before the days of "women's rights," too.

The Subscriber being apprehensive that her Husband, JOHN BROOKS, will contract debts on her account—this is to forbid any person trusting him on her account, as she will not satisfy any debt so contracted after this date—altho my compassion for him is such, that he shall not want for any thing I can help him to—knowing him to be a poor, forlorn young man. I cannot but pity his condition, and sincerely hope he will alter his way of life for the better—tear jealousy from his heart—bury in oblivion his unhappy temper—and take up a firm resolution, that he will turn from the error of his ways, to a better course of life, become a good citizen, a friend to his wife and children, and not hearken any more to his supposed friends (tho greatest enemies)—this is the sincere wish of the Subscriber.

SARAH BROOKS.

Marblehead, March 27, 1793.

In the "Salem Gazette," Oct. 8, 1793, Frederick Jordis complains of "a certain greedy worshipper of Plutus."

Whereas a certain greedy worshipper of Plutus has attempted (canker worm like) to blast the tender bloom of my reputation, by misrepresenting an occurrence that took place between us on the third inst.—I take this method, as the most salutary remedy, to put a stop to its dangerous ravages. I will confess candidly every particular. Sometime since, this man came to me with an account I had in vain demanded of him 4 months ago for horse-hire; having compared it with my own memorandum, I found three charges over and above what I owed him, and the remainder a third higher than usual; finding him unwilling to diminish his unjust claim, I repaired to his house last Thursday to settle with him, and paid him in full the amount of his bill, subtraction made of his three charges: Perceiving his intention was to make me pay them again, I pocketed the bill; his pugilistick arguments to get it back again made me obstinately refuse it; and thanks to a gentleman then present, I escaped his dirty hands. Unwilling to enter the field of Themis with such an antagonist, I will place his receipted account into any impartial man's hands, and submit cheerfully to his decision.

FREDERICK JORDIS.

To show how factories were supplied with operatives in the early days of manufacturing in New England, we copy an advertisement from the "Columbian Centinel," March 4, 1795. This is addressed especially to those parents "who can ill afford to maintain their children." How much better off our manufacturing towns would be if such a system were practicable now!

An exceeding good opportunity for

parents (in these very expensive times for every necessary of life) to provide their children with good and comfortable maintenance, cloathing, schooling, and a trade, but little known and understood in this country.

Mr. Erving proposes to receive as Apprentices to the Cotton and Woolen Manufactory (now going on at New-Haven) any number of Boys or Girls, from the age of ten to fourteen. They will be instructed in all the various branches of the factory, well cloathed and fed, and taught to read, write and cypher; and parents may be assured that the most particular attention will be paid to the morals, as well as to the education, of their children.

Those who can but ill afford to maintain their children, have now an opportunity of binding them to a trade which must, in a few years, be peculiarly beneficial to them and advantageous to their country.

Mr. Erving will thank those that have an inclination to put their children out, to call on him, at his house, No. 42 Marlborough-street, Boston, where they can be more particularly informed of the nature of the factory, and the advantages which must eventually accrue to their children from a general knowledge of this useful branch of business.

March 4, 1795.

THE following lines were written in the Shop of the Subscriber, by a son of St. Crispin, viewing with contempt the tyrannical and oppressive disposition of a Man who has threat'ned vengeance on his neighbour's business, because the article he deals in is SHOES.

Salem, 9th Mo. 6th, 1801.

Oh Shame! that Man a Dog should imitate,
And only live, his fellow Man to hate.
An envious Dog, once in a manger lay,
And starv'd himself, to keep an Ox from hay,
Altho' thereof he could not eat—
Yet if the Ox was starv'd, to him 'twas sweet.
His neighbor's comfort thus for to annoy,
Altho' thereby he did his own destroy.
Oh! Man, such actions from the page erase,
And from thy breast malicious envy CHACE.

☞ Twenty per Cent was struck off at one clip, from those kind of Shoes, which are mostly worn. It is fifteen months since the Shoe War commenced.

J. MANSFIELD, 3d.

A general Assortment of Shoes for Sale as usual, at a living profit.

Salem Register.

Appropriate Mourning.

In consequence of the late afflicting event of the death of the much lamented General Hamilton, TUCKER and THAYER will sell their black ITALIAN CRAPE at the reduced price of one dollar per yard 4-4 wide:—

"GOD takes the Good, too good on earth to stay,
"And leaves the Bad, too bad to take away!"

Columbian Centinel, July 25, 1804.

Bad effects of the abolition of slavery in Providence, R.I.

From the Providence Gazette.

Messrs. Printers,

You will oblige a number of your customers, by publishing the following advertisement in the next Gazette.

Five Hundred Dollars Reward.

Was mislaid, or taken away by mistake (soon after the formation of the Abolition Society) from the Servant Girls of this town, all inclination to do any kind of work;—and left in lieu thereof, an impudent appearance, a strong and continued thirst for high wages, a gossiping disposition for all sorts of amusement, a leering and hankering after persons of the other sex, a desire of finery and fashion, a never ceasing trot after new places more advantageous for stealing—with number of contingent accomplishments that do not suit the wearers. Now if any person or persons will restore to the owners that degree of Honesty and Industry, which has been for some time missing, he or they shall receive the reward of Five Hundred Dollars, beside the warmest blessings of many abused and insulted

HOUSEHOLDERS.

Providence, Oct. 14, 1796.

Parents in Boston cautioned against thorn-apples in "Columbian Centinel," Oct. 26, 1793.

CAUTION!

The Inspector of Police, respectfully makes known to Parents and others, that of late, several children have very much injured themselves, by eating the seeds of Stramonium, or Thorn-Apple, commonly called Devil's Apple; who must inevitably have died, had they not been speedily relieved by Emetics, andc. As those bushes are in several parts of the town, it would be well, if they were destroyed.

Rabbits a curiosity in 1798.

Curious Living Animals.

Mr. Gilbert informs the Public that he has purchased, at considerable expense, a Collection of Living Animals, harmless and playful.

A large Baboon, which is allowed to be the most curious Animal of its kind, ever seen in America.

A Porcupine, Bear, Rackoon and Rabbit, which are also very great curiosities.

☞ The Collection may be seen every day (except Sundays) from 4 o'clock in the afternoon until sunset, at the Granary, head of the Mall, Boston. Admittance Nine Pence for Ladies and Gentlemen, and half price for Children.

May 12.

Columbian Centinel.

Mourning badge for Washington.

A very ingenious and elegant mourning Vignette, stamped on sattin ribbon, for the purpose of being worn by the Ladies on public occasions, is for sale at Mr. Thomas Brewer's shop in Cornhill. The device contains a profile bust of the deceased WASHINGTON in an obelisk, with the trophies of war, and the arms of the U.S.; round the monument are nymphs in the posture of mourning; and on the base are inscribed in legible characters the initials of his name, and the date of his birth and death.

E. Russell's Gazette, Jan. 16, 1800.

Temple of Fame in Boston, with a real eagle, in 1800.

Temple of Fame.

Mr. Bowen respectfully informs the public that the Museum is again opened, with additions and improvements. An excellent figure of GEN. WASHINGTON will appear in a Temple of Fame, expressive of the late melancholy event.—The Young Ladies which represent the Sister States (with a real Eagle hovering over) will be seen with suitable alterations:— with a variety of rural decorations of Groves and Forests.

Jan. 2.

Boston Gazette.

Families used to live in State Street, Boston, in 1796.

☞ A Family in State-street, that does not make a business of keeping boarders, will accommodate a couple of gentlemen, who are disposed to make themselves agreeable in a private family. Apply at the office of the Daily Advertiser.

Daily Advertiser and Polar Star, Dec. 22.

Copley's paintings at auction in 1790.

THIS DAY, (At TEN in the Morning,)

Will be sold by PUBLIC VENDUE at

Russell and Clap's Auction-Room,

COURT STREET,

A Variety of elegant paintings, andc.—principally by the ingenious Mr. Copley.—Also, an Electrical Machine, a glass Case for a shop, andc.

Columbian Centinel, Aug. 31.

The way they compromised with creditors in 1806.

To the Public.

Whereas by misfortunes, together with expenses of law suits, with honest pride I acknowledge I am not worth one cent in the world, and of course cannot pay my debts. But through the assistance of friends, I am now accommodated with a Shop, and necessary Tools to carry on my business, in Cambridge-Port; where I shall be happy to execute any kind of work for those I am indebted to, at the lowest cash price, on this condition—that I am paid one half of what the work comes to, in cash, when delivered. But if my creditors will allow me time, and my health is spared, I have no doubt I shall soon be able to pay twenty shillings on the pound to them, in cash.

To those gentlemen I am not indebted to, I solicit of them a share of their work, assuring them, that whatever engagements I make, shall be executed punctually, and in a workmanlike manner, by their humble servant,
RICHARD GRIDLEY.
Cambridge-Port, sept. 10, 1806.

☞ The Printers of Newspapers in Boston are requested to publish the above, provided they will receive their pay in Smith's work.
Columbian Centinel.
On the 11th of January, 1799, Mr. Briggs advertises in the "Salem Gazette" and thanks "the good people of the County of Essex for their spirited exertions in bringing down the trees of the forest for building the frigate. In the short space of four weeks, the full complement of timber has been furnished." He ends by saying:—
"Next September is the time
When we'll launch her from the strand,
And our cannon load and prime
With tribute due to Talleyrand."
The following advertisement appeared in the papers in 1798, in reference to the building of the frigate "Essex":—
THE
Salem   Salem Frigate   Frigate.
TAKE NOTICE!
Ye Sons of Freedom! all true lovers of the Liberty of your Country! step forth, and give your assistance in building the Frigate, to oppose French insolence and piracy. Let every man in possession of a White Oak Tree, be ambitious to be foremost in hurrying down the timber to Salem, and fill the complement wanting, where the noble structure is to be fabricated, to maintain your rights upon the Seas, and make the name of America respected among the nations of the world. Your largest and longest trees are wanted, and the arms of them for Knees and Rising Timber. Four trees are wanted for the Keel, which all together will measure 146 feet in length, and hew 16 inches square. Please to call on the Subscriber, who wants to make contracts for large or small quantities, as may suit best, and will pay the READY CASH.
ENOS BRIGGS.
Salem, Nov. 23, 1798.
CASH GIVEN FOR
One ton COPPER, in pigs, or old COPPER—10 tons best old Sable or Swedes IRON. Apply to the Subscriber.
Also—WANTED,
A Blacksmith, to contract for doing all the IRON WORK of the
SALEM FRIGATE.
*** Proposals therefor, will be received from any Smith, sealed and directed

to
JOHN JENKS.
Salem, Nov. 21.
In the "Gazette" of Oct. 1, 1799, appears the following brief account of the launching of the "Essex;" also a communication in reference to the frigate.
Salem,
Tuesday, October 1, 1799.
Yesterday the FRIGATE ESSEX, of 32 guns, was launched from the stocks, in this town. She went into the water with the most easy and graceful motion, amidst the acclamations of thousands of spectators, and a federal salute from her guns on the hill, returned by an armed ship in the harbour, commanded by Capt. Thomas Williams. The Committee acting for the subscribers, Col. Hacket, the superintendant, and Mr. Briggs, the master builder, have thus the satisfaction of producing to their country as fine a ship, of her size, as graces the American Navy. It is not yet known who will command her; but it is on all hands agreed that she is well calculated to do essential service to her country.
COMMUNICATION.
And ADAMS said, "Let there be a Navy!"
and there was a Navy.
To build a Navy was the advice of our venerable sage. How far it has been adhered to, is demonstrated by almost every town in the United States, that is capable of floating a galley or a gun boat.
Salem has not been backward in this laudable design. Impressed with a due sense of the importance of a Navy, the patriotic citizens of this town put out a subscription, and thereby obtained an equivalent for building a vessel of force. Among the foremost in this good work were Messrs. Derby and Gray, who set the example by subscribing ten thousand dollars each. But alas! the former is no more—we trust his good deeds follow him.
Such was the patriotic zeal with which our citizens were impressed, that in the short space of SIX MONTHS they contracted for the materials and equipment of a Frigate of 32 guns, and had her completed yesterday for launching. The chief part of the timber was standing but six months ago—and in a moment, as it were, "every Grove descended," to put in force the patriotic intentions of those at whose expense she was built.
Yesterday the Stars and Stripes were unfurled on board the Frigate ESSEX, and at 12 o'clock she made a majestic movement into her destined element, there to join her sister craft in repelling foreign aggressions, and maintaining the Rights and Liberties of a "Great, Free, Powerful and Independent Nation."
The concourse of spectators was immense; and the averted face of jacobinism was not seen depicted on the countenance of a single one;—but on the contrary, the heart-felt satisfaction of the beholders of this

magnificent spectacle, was evinced by the concording shouts and huzzas of thousands, which reiterated from every quarter.

The unremitting zeal of Mr. Briggs, the Architect of this beautiful ship, cannot be too highly applauded. His assiduity, in bringing her into a state of such perfection, in so short a time, entitles him to the grateful thanks of his country; and we fondly hope that his labours have not been spent in vain, for we may truly say that he has not given rest to the sole of his foot, since her keel was first laid.

The "Massachusetts Mercury," Dec. 27, 1799, says:—

The frigate Essex, of 32 guns, capt. Prebble, sailed from Salem on Sunday morning last for Newport. She saluted Fort Pickering, which returned the salute. She sails remarkably well.

At "No. 1, Honesty Side," Salem, dry goods were to be had in 1807.

John H. Keith

Informs the inhabitants of Salem and its environs, that on the 15th day of April next ensuing, he intends opening a Shop for the purpose of vending

Dry Goods,

No 1, Honesty Side.

Constantly for Sale, American, French, English, Italian, Dutch and India manufactures, from the coarse Tow Cloth to the fine Cobweb Muslin.— Said Keith will attend personally from the sun's oriental ascension to its occidental declination.—To prevent a superfluity of words, he observes that there will be only one price for his goods at retail, and another for wholesale, and that cash will be the staple commodity receivable at his bank. Bills of any of the States will be received, provided the stockholders are known to be good and responsible men.

March 24.

Salem Gazette, April 3.

The "Worcester Spy" in 1797 had the following quaint advertisement:—

Honesty is the best Policy.

The Gentleman Night Walker, alias Night Villain, who of late has frequented the SLAUGHTER HOUSE of Lemuel Rice, and taken therefrom a considerable quantity of FRESH BEEF, is informed, that if he comes forward, in a gentleman like manner, and settles for the same, his name shall not be exposed; but, if he neglects this friendly hint, he must shortly expect to be complimented by a WARRANT, which will give him that reward his LABORS justly merit.

Worcester, April 5th, 1797.

The "Grand Lodge." Paul Revere, master, has the following notice in the "Massachusetts Centinel:"—

Grand Lodge.

The Officers and Members of the GRAND LODGE, and the Representatives of Lodges, are hereby requested to attend a Quarterly

Communication at Concert-Hall in Boston, on the evening of Monday, the 9th March, at 7 o'clock.

By order of the Most Worshipful

PAUL REVERE, G. Master.

DANIEL OLIVER, G. Secretary.

Boston, Feb. 28, 5795.

A remarkable dog is on exhibition in Salem, March 24, 1807.

THE SAPIENT DOG.

AT WASHINGTON-HALL,

To-Morrow Evening.

The extraordinary sagacity of this Animal, supercedes the necessity of puffing advertisements or exaggerated bills—that the Sapient Dog is a great curiosity, the Proprietor feels no hesitation in affirming, that his feats of activity are more various and pleasing than any preceding exhibition of a similar nature, all of which will be made manifest to every spectator, by his dexterity and precision in exhibiting the following performances—viz.

He illuminates the Exhibition Room, himself, by Lighting
his own Lamps.

By means of Typographical Cards, (in the same manner
as a Printer composes,)

He Spells, and Reads Print or Writing.

By any person's watch in the company,

Tells the time of the Day,

Both the hour and minutes—the date of the year, day of the month, and week, and distinguishes colours.

As an Arithmetician,

He Adds, Subtracts, Divides and Multiplies,

Tells how many persons there are present,

Discharges a loaded Cannon, and jumps through a Hoop.

To conclude—the proprietor will suffer any Lady or Gentleman in the company, to make choice of a card, and the Dog, notwithstanding the face of both packs are concealed from him, will discover the card so drawn.

☞ Tickets at 25 cents, to be sold at Cushing and Appleton's Book-Store, children half price.—No money received at the door.

Gazette.

The "Shaksperian Society" of Boston has "new revised" articles in 1795, according to the following notice to members:—

Shaksperian Society.

Take Notice—All persons who have regularly been balloted for, as Members of the above Society, who have not yet signed the Articles, since their being new revised, must attend this Evening, and execute the same, or they will not be admitted as Members thereof. Members of the above society are requested to attend early on particular business.

By Order,
J. ROBINSON, Sec'y.
March 7, 1795.
Connecticut "Election Goods."
The Subscriber refers the generous Public to his late advertisements to be informed of the articles he still continues to sell by wholesale and retail; and also respectfully informs them, that he has just come to hand, a fresh assortment of Chintzes and Callicoes, Gentlemen's fancy Waistcoating, silk Romal, buff and other Shawls, printed Jeans, cotton and linen Handkerchiefs, a variety of Ribbons, all of a late importation; Nankeens of a superior quality, and cheaper by nine pence in the single piece than can be purchased in New-York by the quantity. Among his fancy patterns for ladies are, the Covent Garden Cross-bar, the Renelagh full moon, the Prussian stormont, Harlequin's motto, and an olive check inclosing four lions rampant and three flours de Luce; and for gentlemen's waistcoating, the Sportsman's fancy, the Prince of Wales's New-Market jockey, and the modest pale blue. He doubts not in the least, but that among the great variety of figures he has, every fancy may be suited; and as for the prices, he makes not the least hesitation to assert, they will be approved.—He also has taken the greatest pains to procure for young masters and misses such cloths and figures as will be durable, pleasing, and well suited to the approaching general election.
THOMAS TISDALL.
N.B. A few pair of gentlemen's doe skin hunting Gloves, and choice old Spirits by the gallon; a little of which may be used as a cordial.
9
Hartford, next door south of Mess. Hudson }
and Goodwin's Printing-Office, 1788.
The crooked Staff of Life.
Pure, mild and unadulterated St. CROIX RUM, to be sold by the hogshead, barrel or lesser quantity, on pleasing terms, for one of the great essentials, Solid Coin, by the public's very humble servant, next door to Hudson and Goodwin's Printing-Office.
THOMAS TISDALE.
Connecticut Courant, May 19, 1788.
Republican BEEF.
The subscriber respectfully informs the citizens of Hartford, that he has purchased the fattest OX and COW perhaps in Connecticut, which will be killed and ready for sale for the ensuing Election, at a low price for the times. Those who wish to purchase real good Beef, will please to apply to
WILLIAM BROWN.
April 28, 1794.
Connecticut Courant.

Nantucket wit and humor on the 4th of July, in the year 1829.

A Grand Touch. The last Nantucket Inquirer contains the following advertisement:—

At the sign of the Eastern Pine,

Where the red and the white combine.

John Peters, a descendant of the famous English Divine, Hugh Peters, informs all the tidy citizens of Nantucket, that Apollo and the Graces came over in the last packet, and have taken up their abode at the corner of Pearl and Water streets. He officiates as high Priest in their temple, where it is his delightful task to adorn the outward man, to shave off excrescences, and trim into proportion the shrubbery which nature has reared around the headpieces of mankind.—By a judicious application of the scissors of discrimination, the soap of good nature, the brush of reform, and the razor of decision, he expects to bring about results which, like powers of the Steam Engine are, as yet, only dreamed of. The grace of the Athenian beau and the dignity of the Roman senator shall be so intermingled in the grand contour of all who submit to his touch, that the toute ensemble cannot fail to kindle love and command respect.

CHARLES HARDY,

STREET SWEEPER,

Takes this method publicly to return his grateful thanks to his friends of Marlborough street, Cornhill, andc. for their kindness to him during the past season; not only in patronizing him while able to perform his usual labors, but in assisting him while under the influence of a distressing and debilitating disease. He has grown old in the service of the inhabitants of Boston, and they do not forget him—they do not cast him off, or suffer him to become an inmate of the Alms-house; and although he is an African, he will not be guilty of the blackest of sins—that of ingratitude. He humbly solicits a continuance of their favors, to enable him to buffet the inclemency of the approaching season, (when his regular employment fails) and flatters himself he shall still be able to sustain that character of fidelity which the partiality of his friends has bestowed upon him.

Boston, Nov. 28, 1815.

Columbian Centinel.

The subscriber wishes to notify his old honourable customers, who practise stealing and destroying his fruit every year, that his Water Mellons are now almost ripe; and if they do not as usual destroy the fruit and vines immediately, they will get entirely ripe; and then some body or other will be the better for them, which will be a grievous mortification to those manly gentlemen.

EZRA GRISWOLD.

Simsbury, August 4, 1794.

Connecticut Courant.

Removal.

SAMUEL MYLOD informs his friends and the public that he has removed from Danvers to the building belonging to Mrs. Martha Procter, near Buffum's corner, Salem, where he colours all kinds of wearing apparel. Silks cleansed from spots or injury from sea. N.B. Pickles that will keep the longest voyage, for Sale.

Oct. 11.*

Salem Gazette, 1805.

In "old times" even publishers were sometimes short of money, and ready to barter with their subscribers. So celebrated a character as Isaiah Thomas, of the "Worcester Spy," was occasionally obliged to give "hints" to his "Delinquent Customers and Postriders." The latter were distributers of papers to country customers.

To Delinquent Customers.

☞Serious Times—or the Printer without Money—or a Final Hint to Delinquent Customers and Postriders!☜

The Subscriber has frequently given

Hints to his Delinquent Customers and Postriders, that he was in want of Cash and has repeatedly invited all indebted to him to come forward and make an immediate settlement, without being put to any extra cost—he now, for the last time, informs all that are indebted to him for Newspapers, Advertisements, andc. andc. that an immediate settlement must be made, and all who disregard this notice, may depend upon having their Notes and Accounts put into the hands of an Attorney.

To accommodate those who cannot pay money, the following articles will be received until the FIRST of JANUARY, 1803, viz. Corn, Rye, Wheat, Oats, and Wood—Those who have not the above articles, and who cannot make it convenient to pay the money at present, their NOTES will be received, payable in Three Months, provided they are given previous to the Second Wednesday in March next.

ISAIAH THOMAS, Jun.

Worcester, November 17, 1802.

To be SOLD,

And entered upon next April,

The House and Land now occupied by the subscriber, pleasently situated at a very public corner, in the main street, at the West part of the town.——After serving the public faithfully, for several years, as a private soldier in the army, and suffering most intolerable hardships, I am now, on account of my country's unfaithfulness, in not paying what they owe me, obliged to sell the house which belonged to my ancestors, in order to pay my debts, and to retire to an obscure hut at some distance from the town.

JOSEPH METCALF.

Salem Gazette, 1784.

An advertisement like the following is not only "quaint or curious," but it is also rare:—

One evening last week, a piece of Gold was passed, through mistake, at Beverly Ferry, to Asa Leech's Ferryman, with coppers, for a copper.——— The owner may have it again, applying to said Leech, telling the marks, and paying the charges.

Beverly, Sept. 20, 1784.

Salem Gazette.

In 1798 a "Learned Pig" was in Salem, and we notice that about the same time a learned dog was exhibited.

For ten days only.

Mr. PINCHBECK

Respectfully informs the Inhabitants of SALEM, that he has just arrived in this town with that great natural curiosity, the

Pig of Knowledge,

And flatters himself, after exhibiting before the President

of the United States with unbounded applause,

and in every principal City in the Union,

to have the honour of gratifying

such Ladies and Gentlemen

in this place, as may

favour him with their

Company.

This extraordinary Animal will actually perform the following surprising particulars, viz.

He reads print or writing, spells, tells the time of day, both the hours and minutes, by any person's watch in the company, the date of the year, the day of the month, distinguishes colours, how many persons there are present, ladies or gentlemen, and to the astonishment of every spectator, will answer any question in the four first rules of Arithmetick. To conclude, any Lady or Gentleman may draw a card from a pack, and keep it concealed, and the PIG without hesitation will discover the card when drawn.

Those who doubt the truth of the above are informed in case it don't answer every expectation the advertisement can excite, and prove a real living Animal, shall have the Money returned, or be at liberty to pay after they have convinced themselves by seeing him perform.

To be seen in a convenient room under the western side of Concert-Hall, Market-Street.

Admittance, for grown persons, one Quarter of a Dollar.——Children half price.

N.B. Strict attention paid to keep the place fit for the reception of Ladies.

MAY 4, 1798.

Salem Gazette.

This is a quiet way of asking a favor; taken from a paper of 1811:—

☞ Mr. Lang would thank the person that took a Camblet Cloak from his entry the last summer to return it, as he expects to want it the approaching cold weather.

Mr. George W. Felt seems not to have been accustomed to show much gallantry, judging from his notice in the "Salem Gazette," Sept. 4, 1804.

WHEREAS two GIRLS were seen taking APPLES from the Subscriber's Field, on Sunday last, in North Fields, so called, if they will call and settle for the same, THIS DAY, they will avoid further trouble!

GEORGE W. FELT.

Salem, Sept. 4, 1804.

Females seem to have been often in difficulty in "old times," as appears from some of the advertisements, of which we give a few specimens. But perhaps this was due in part, at least, to "kleptomania,"—a disease then but little understood.

☞ The FEMALE, who a few days since took 4 Pair of SLIPPERS from a shop in old Paved Street, is requested to return them, and no questions will be asked; if she does not return them in 6 days she will hear from the owner another way.

Jan. 5, 1792.

The Female who offered a Counterfeit Seven Dollar Bill at Mr. Dow's Shop, on Wednesday afternoon, and afterwards passed it upon a small Lad at another shop, is desired to call and exchange the same, if she wishes to avoid trouble, as her name is known.

Nov. 1, 1805.

The Female that took from the Shop of the subscriber on Monday, 19th of June, four pair COTTON HOSE, is requested to return them to prevent further exposure.

June 20, 1815.

JOHN RUST.

An indiscreet and ungrateful servant advertised as missing. We take the following from the "Columbian Centinel," Sept. 30, 1807:—

A GOOD LIKENESS OF SANCHO, A NEGRO MAN,

thirty years of age, about 5 feet high, very black complexion, good teeth, not corpulent, but well formed, and of erect position of body and a fast walker, WHO absented himself (supposed to have been inveigled away by some artful villains for their own use and benefit) upon the Evening of the 17th inst. from his Master, Winthrop Sargent, late Governor of the Missisippi Territory. He had learned the trade of a Barber, and is in every respect a most accomplished servant for a gentleman or a family; was born and educated in his Master's house; endeared to him, his mistress, and his own wife and children, as well as the numerous blacks of his Master's Plantations, by long, affectionate, and faithful services, and ere this solitary instance of malconduct, there was not a single doubt entertained that the attachments were mutual and inviolable. If he voluntarily returns to the service of his Master, he shall be received with wonted kindness and affection, but no expense will be spared to punish to the utmost limits of the law, all persons who may be accessory in harboring or concealing him, and the sum of FIFTY DOLLARS shall be paid to any person who will apprehend and deliver him to his Master, or in his absence to Mr. Ignatius Sargent, in Boston; to Messrs. G. and T. Aspinwalle, in New-York; or Col. Hodgdon, in Philadelphia;—or the sum of ONE HUNDRED DOLLARS for delivering him to Mr. David Urquhart, Merchant, New-Orleans.

WINTHROP SARGENT.

UNGUIOLOGY.

Just Received, and for Sale at the Printing-Office of BELCHER and ARMSTRONG, No. 79, State-street, and at the several Bookstores—a few copies of that rare and valuable work, "A Translation of Doctor Gasper Gall La'Veytur's UNGUIOLOGY, or the doctrine of Toe-Nails." The various editions, languages, and countries, through which this publication has passed almost in rapid succession, exceed calculation. Gentlemen of literature are invited to apply in season, as the work is under restriction and cannot be reprinted in this country. Foreign reviews speaking of it say, "The ingenuity of Doctor Gasper Gall La'Veytur's Unguiological system exceeds the capacity of our praise. It is impossible for any one of judgment and penetration to read this work without being convinced that the seat of the soul is in the toe-nails; the superior advantages which this index has over physiognomy and craniology are made most incontrovertibly evident to the most common comprehension." Price 32-1/2 cents. august 27.

Centinel, 1806.

The really curious collection of the Columbian Museum is advertised in the "Boston Chronicle," Dec. 19, 1797.

LATE ADDITIONS TO THE

COLUMBIAN MUSEUM,

At the Head of the MALL, Boston.

Mr. BOWEN informs the Public, that he has purchased Mr. PAFF's much admired Exhibition of

CONCERT CLOCKS,

Which are placed at the head of the Museum Hall, as a valuable and pleasing addition to that very extensive repository of CURIOSITIES.

1. A canary bird, which sings a variety of beautiful songs, minuets, marches, andc. natural as life. 2. A company of Automatum Figures, which dance to the Music of an Harpsichord. 3. Three Figures, which play the Organ and

Clarinet in concert. 4. Three Figures, which play the Harpsichord and Hautboys, in concert. 5. King Herod beheading John the Baptist, and his Daughter holding a charger to receive the head. 6. A Chimney Sweep and his boy on the top of a chimney. 7. Three Figures which strike the hours and quarters. 8. A Butcher killing an Ox.

The above CONCERT CLOCKS have been exhibited in New-York, with universal applause, and are well worthy the attention of the Citizens of Boston and the Public in general.

The Musuem also contains the most extensive Collection of

ELEGANT PAINTINGS,

That ever was exhibited in the United States, some of which are 10 by 12 feet, elegantly framed, and valued from 500 to 1000 dols.

ALSO—A Collection of upwards of

50 elegant Figures of WAXWORK, Large as Life, among which are the following (the most interesting) viz.

The late King of France, taking an affectionate leave of his family just before he suffered under the guillotine: The Queen appears in a rage of distraction—the King's Sister deeply affected—the young Princess is fainting—and the Dauphin is embracing his unhappy Father—the Queen's Maid of Honor also appears in great distress. A guard of Soldiers are waiting to conduct him to the place of execution. This is an affecting scene which appears as natural as the life, and is the most interesting group of WAX FIGURES that ever was exhibited to the United States.

GEORGE WASHINGTON, late President of the United States, is elegantly situated in the centre of the Museum Hall, surrounded by four beautiful Wax Figures, representing LIBERTY, with the staff and cap—JUSTICE, with the sword and balance—PEACE, with the olive branch extended and PLENTY, with a cornucopia, or horn of plenty, loaded with fruit.

Dr. FRANKLIN, sitting at a table, with the late Dr. STILES, President of Yale College, Connecticut. The New-York Beauty. The Sleeping Nymph. A Tea Party of Young Ladies, with a Servant Negro Girl. The Salem Beauty. Maternal Affection, or a Lady with two beautiful Children. The Boston Beauty. Sir Charles Grandison and Miss Harriet Byron. Charlotte weeping at the Tomb of Werter.—Humphreys and Mendoza, the celebrated English Boxers. The domestic Cottager, at the spinning wheel. The venerable John S. Hutton, who lately died in Philadelphia, aged 108 years and 4 months, drest with the same cloathes which he wore when living, with his own cane, pipe, tobacco-box, andc. The assassination of MARAT, by the beautiful Miss CHARLOTTE CORDE, in France. Two Greenwich Pensioners. The late unfortunate Baron TRENCK, loaded with large iron chains in a real Prison. An Indian Warrior, with his tomahawk, belts of wampum, andc. Two Chinese Mandarines, drest in the modern stile of that country. Also,

two Mandarines, deposited in the Museum, For Sale.
With a great variety of
Natural and Artificial Curiosities;
Among which are a great variety of Birds, live Owls, Beasts, Reptiles, Serpents, (one of which is a Rattle-Snake, 9 years of age, and 4 feet in length,) Insects, Diamond Beetle, Glass Frigates, two feet in length, compleatly rigged and mounted with Glass Guns, andc.
The MUSEUM has lately received the principal Additions for this season— It is Opened Every Day, (except Sundays) and ILLUMINATED every Tuesday, Thursday, and Friday Evenings.
Notice to the economical, from the "Salem Mercury," July 8, 1788.

☞ Save your Rags!
And send them to the Printing Office; you will there receive for what you think of no service, money enough, which, in effect, is the same as having money for nothing, and is certainly better than to be at the trouble of sweeping Rags away. If this beloved argument is thought insufficient to procure them, then only think of the virtue of serving your country!
"Beauties" to be seen.
New Additions.
The BOSTON MUSEUM, North side the Market, has lately received many very valuable additions, among which are
The Philadelphia, New-York, and Salem Beauties, and a number of other Figures.—Also, a variety of natural curiosities, among which are the skin of the Sea-Elephant, in natural preservation, which measures 8 feet in length, and 6 feet round the body, andc. The skin of the African Lion, a Calf with 8 legs, 2 bodies, and one head, in natural preservation, andc. andc.
Museum opened every day and evening, Saturdays and Sundays excepted.

☞ Admittance to the Museum, 25 Cents.
The Invisible Lady, and Acoustic Temple, continues to be exhibited among the other curiosities, at 25 Cents admittance.
June 29.
Columbian Centinel, 1805.
A case of short weight of a load of hay is gravely advertised in the "Columbian Centinel" by the town-weigher
Mr. RUSSELL,
THIS day came Ezekiel Kingsbury, jun., of Dedham, with a Load of Hay to be weighed, which was accordingly done. After it was weighed, he drove it off round Mr. Greenleaf's corner, where he stopped. Mr. Jonathan Trask, truckman, wanted to purchase a load of hay—went and tried to bargain with him for it, and as he was going towards the hay, he perceived a man raise his head on the top of the load, by the name of Draper, of said town. He accordingly came to me and told me of it. I went in pursuit of

Kingsbury, and overtook him just before he got to the Granary, and ordered him back to the scales to have his load weighed again, which weighed one hundred and an half less that it did before.—The several printers are requested to insert the above, to prevent further impositions on the publick.

HOPESTILL FOSTER, Hay-weigher.

Boston, Dec. 15, 1789.

It seems to have been the fashion in "old times" with people who had articles stolen from them to advertise in the papers, requesting the thief or thieves to make restitution. Probably this was the surest method of recovery, in the absence of the detective system. Joseph Tyler in the "Boston Gazette," Nov. 21, 1761, is inclined to be sarcastic, and Samuel Brazer, of Worcester, in 1802, is witty, but modest. As to stealing psalm-books, no one would dream of doing such a thing in these days. Our modern thieves are not interested in devotional books; they prefer "yellow-covered literature."

Joseph Tyler desires the Person

that borrowed his Surtout to return it, if it is not worn out.

1767.

Taken out of the Pew, No. 59,

in the Rev'd Mr. Barnard, senior's Meeting-House, about a Month since, a PSALM-BOOK. The Person is desired to return it, otherwise may depend upon being exposed.

Essex Gazette, Sept. 28, 1773.

A MODEST REQUEST!

The two obliging Ladies, who on the night of Monday, the 29th ultimo, between six and seven o'clock in the evening, took from the Store of the Subscriber (not by mistake) FIVE BARCELONA HANDKERCHIEFS, are desired to return them immediately, with satisfactory remuneration, or the next notice they receive will come "GREETING."

SAMUEL BRAZER.

Worcester, December 8, 1802.

The person who took six pair of SHOES, one day last week, under a false name, from a shop in Essex Street, would do well, if they wish to avoid difficulties, to return them immediately.

Salem, July 22.

Salem Gazette, 1800.

The Person who yesterday, at dusk, took a piece of black VELVET from the shop board of the Subscribers, is well known. He has now an opportunity of returning it, and if not immediately done, shall suffer the penalty of the Law.

J. and I. NEWHALL.

Salem, Nov. 5, 1805.

Pictures like the following could be seen in the "Essex Gazette" in 1771 (May 14).

Ran away from the Subscriber,

on the 4th of May, a Negro Man named Cato, of a middling Stature, has lost the Sight of his left Eye, had on a kersey Jacket and leather Breeches. Whoever shall take up said Negro, and bring him to his Master in Salem, shall have Two Dollars Reward, and all Charges paid, by

William Hunt.

Vessels were accommodated at "Rotting Row," in Salem, in 1812, and we presume there is room for some now.

Several BIRTHS for VESSELS are vacant at Rotting Row, the tides are favorable and the Dockage so extremely low, good and safe, as to make it an object for any one to haul his vessel there to winter.

Salem, Nov. 20.

It used to be common in the early part of this century to see such goods as "Mamoodies," "Chittabully Baftas," etc., advertised in the Salem and Boston papers.

JOHN STONE,

Has for sale,

Front street,

ONE bale MUGGA MAMOODIES;

1 do. MADRAS PAT HANDKERCHIEFS;

1 do. ALEABAD MOWSANNAS;

1 do. do. MAMODIES;

1 do. CHITTABULLY BAFTAS;

1 do. JOLLOPOUR SANNAS;

1 do. BANDANNAS;

Imported in the ship Union, Capt. Osgood, from Calcutta, and of the first chop.

Sept. 24, 1811.

In another advertisement we notice "Guzzenahs, Allebad Emerty, Taundah Khassah, Mahge Gunge." These are all India cottons.

It seems strange to us now, when we see so many boot-blacks everywhere, to learn that in 1815 the "craft" advertised in the papers, as did "wood-sawyers," too, about the same time. As coal had not then been introduced into Salem, everybody burned wood, so that wood-sawing was an occupation of considerable importance. During the war of 1813 wood became rather scarce, and some people used dried turf, or peat, as it was called, for fuel.

Boots and Shoes Cleaned.

York MORRIS respectfully informs the Gentlemen of Salem, that he has taken the Shop one door west of the Sun Tavern, where he will be happy to clean their Boots and Shoes in the best manner, and at the shortest notice.——He will keep constantly for sale LIQUID BLACKING of a very superior quality, in jugs and bottles. Also, a Composition, with which he cleans Ladies' Walking Shoes.

April 18.

This York Morris was father of the Boston colored lawyer, Robert Morris.

Boots and Shoes Cleaned.

Thomas JONES respectfully informs the Gentlemen of Salem, that he has taken the Shop (recently occupied by York Morris) two doors west of the Sun Tavern, where he will be happy to clean their BOOTS and SHOES in the best manner, and at the shortest notice.

Salem, June 13.

Wood-Sawing.

The Subscriber, being under the interdict of a Non-Intercourse law, his horses and waggons hauled into dry dock, will no longer carry freight between Salem and Boston; but, "abandoning the ocean altogether," he respectfully offers his services to his federal friends, with his saw and wooden horse, and shall be obliged to them to call upon him when they have any wood to cut. Orders will be received at his dwelling, near the Court-house.

JOHN L. MATTHEWS.

☞ Wanted to hire—two smart men. June 11 [1811].

Specific for a "religious hydrophobia" in 1819.

Cochranism Delineated,

Or a description of, and specific for, a religious Hydrophobia, which has spread and is still spreading in a number of towns in the counties of York and Cumberland, District of Maine—price 12 1·2 cents—for sale at the Bookstore of

HENRY WHIPPLE.

June 12.

The following is printed in the "Massachusetts Mercury:"—

From the Georgia Gazette.

Vice Consulship of Spain for the States of North Carolina, South Carolina, and Georgia.

Messrs. Nicholas Johnston and Co.

Gentlemen,

His Excellency Lieut. Colonel Don Vincent Folch, Governor of the Province of West Florida, in a letter, dated Panzacola, 1st August, has been pleased to communicate to me the following:

"I have issued a proclamation, offering FOUR THOUSAND FIVE HUNDRED DOLLARS to any person who will deliver here, or in Apalache, the body of WILLIAM AUGUSTUS BOWLES, or else produce sufficient proof of having killed him; which information I will thank you to make public, in order that some clever fellow, at the cheap rate of one gun shot, will place in his pocket the said sum, which shall be paid, with the greatest acknowledgment of gratitude, in good Spanish dollars, without the least delay."

Therefore I request you to give this a conspicuous place in your paper. It is, doubtless, a very interesting subject to Spain, America and the Indians, that they be rid of this noted vagabond.

I remain, with respect,

Your obedient servant,

EMANUEL RENGILL.

Savannah, 25th August, 1800.

Progress of Refinement in America.

INDIANS' SCALPS.

Pittsburg, May 17, 1791.

We the subscribers, encouraged by a large subscription, do promise to pay One Hundred Dollars for every hostile Indian's scalp, with both ears to it,[B] taken between this date and the 15th day of June next, by any inhabitant of Alleghany county.

George Wallace, Robert Elliot,

Wm. Amberson, A. Tannehill,

J. Wilkins, jun. John Irwin.

[B] The shape of the ears, we suppose, is to determine the enmity of the Indian.

Salem Gazette.

A negro "pretends to be very religious." From the "Boston Gazette."

Ran away from me the Subscriber

at Londonderry, in the Province of New-Hampshire, on the 28th of September, a Negro Man Servant named Prince, about Forty Years of Age, about five Feet five Inches high, speaks good English, had on when he went away a green Coat, blue plush Breeches, diaper Jacket, several pair of thread Stockings with him; he looks very serious and grave, and pretends to be very religious: He is the property of Major Rogers, and has been several Years in the Service to the Westward, and pretends to be free.

Whoever will take up said Slave and bring him to me, or to Capt. Jonathan Brewer at Framingham, shall have FIVE DOLLARS Reward and all necessary Charges paid by me,

James Rogers.

Dated at Londonderry, October 8, 1762.

In the "Boston Gazette," Oct. 8, 1759, some servants are advertised who among other accomplishments speak high and low Dutch. At this time two dollars and a half was the value of a pound in New York currency, while the New England currency was three dollars and thirty-three cents to a pound. To this day a shilling is 12-1/2 cents in New York, and in New England 16-2/3 cents.

Run away from Major Edmond Matthis of Albany, in the Province of New-York, the following People, viz. A Servant Man named William Fairfield, of a dark Complection, down look, black Hair, and of a middling Stature. Also a Negro Man and Woman, and a white Girl with them, about 14 Years of Age, who talks good English, high and low Dutch; the Negro Man is much pitted with the Small Pox, and speaks good English; tis suppos'd they are all together: They took with them a great many Cloaths, and its probable they will often alter their Dress. Whoever takes up said Run-aways, and safely conveys them to their abovesaid Master, shall have Ten Pounds (25 Dollars) New-York Currency Reward, and all necessary Charges paid.
Albany, Octob. 1, 1759.
Edmond Matthis.
Dr. Greenwood, of Boston, in 1788 offered his services to "give a youthful air to the countenance," and was ready to "electerise" any persons who stood "in need of that almost universal remedy."
ISAAC GREENWOOD,
DENTIST,
Acquaints the publick, that he has REMOVED from No. 49 to No. 19, Marlborough Street, opposite Messrs. Amorys' Store, where he continues to perform the necessary branches of that art, carefully and faithfully. Removing every substance tending to destroy the Teeth and Gums. Cures the Scurvy in the Gums, makes the Teeth white, andc. Sells BRUSHES that are suitable for the Teeth, with a POWDER that never fails to recommend itself, at 1/4 per box. Fixes NATURAL TEETH on plates of gold or silver, with gold springs, if wanted. Also, substitutes ARTIFICIAL TEETH, of different substances, from 2s. to 6s. each—that give a youthful air to the countenance, and render pronunciation more agreeable and distinct—In a word, both natural and artificial are of such real service, as are worthy the attention of every one. He with pleasure attends on those who may incline to employ him, provided they cannot conveniently attend on him, at his HOUSE, where he has every accommodation necessary for their reception.
At the same place may be had,
Oil, Silk, and Ladies' UMBRELLAS, cheap. Old Umbrellas repaired, oiled, newly covered, andc. Oil Silk CAPS for bathing, German Flutes, Fifes, Violins, and Strings for ditto, Reeds for hautboys, Men, Boxes and Dice for back-gammon, Chess men, Billiard Balls, Ivory Combs, a variety of Canes, by wholesale and retail. Cane Strings, Whips, electrical Machines with apparatus for experiments and medical use—artificial Magnets, andc. andc. andc.
N.B. Said Greenwood offers his service to electerise those who stand in need of that almost universal remedy, at 1/6 each time, at his House.
☞ Advise with your physicians.
May 3, 1788.

REMOVAL.

Boston Umbrella Manufactury.

DANIEL HEWES,

Umbrella Manufacturer; takes this early opportunity to inform his friends and the Public in general, that he has Removed from the North-Square, to No. 55, Marlborough-Street,

at the sign of the Umbrella——where may be had any quantity, quality, or sized UMBRELLAS, at the shortest notice, made of better materials, cheaper, and more durable than can be imported.

Also,

Turned Work in Ivory, hard Woods, and Metals, executed in the best stile of workmanship.

☞ Cash given for Ivory, Sea-horse, and Sea-cows TEETH. (8w)

March 14 [1798].

The following—supposed to be—attempt at wit appeared in the "Massachusetts Centinel" in 1789.

ADVERTISEMENTS EXTRA.

Imported in the last vessels from Europe, A treatise on ogling, simpering, flirting, gigling, painting, patching, perfuming, andc. very useful to every Lady—and much in demand. Also, The Art of burning dimples in ladies' cheeks and chins—of repairing female tongues that wear with using—of setting eyes fashionably in their sockets—of giving the face a beautiful pale, deathlike aspect—and of acquiring the elegant hysterick and other fits.

TO BE SOLD—Many elegant and beautiful copies of a most scarce and valuable work, called "The Virtue of the Times." Inquire any where.

LOST—Through carelessness, thirty good years of life—of a gentleman—ALSO, forty-two years of a lady—the latter, from a desire to appear beautifully slim. Whoever can inform the losers how they can be redeemed, shall be handsomely rewarded.

EXTRA—BUT SERIOUS.

WANTED—much wanted—several small sums of money—say, from 4/6. to Ten Dollars—for which obligations, which have frequently been offered, will be given. Inquire of the Printer.

A Boston paper of 1789 prints the following unique production, copied from a late London paper. It was probably designed as a "take-off" to some of the humbugs of the day.

THOMAS TOUCHWOOD, GENT.,

Proposes, on the last day of the present month, to shoot himself by subscription. His life being of no farther use to himself or his friends, he takes this method of endeavouring to turn his death to some account; and the novelty of the performance, he hopes, will merit the attention and patronage of the publick.

He will perform with two pistols, the first shot to be directed through his abdomen, to which will be added another through his brain, the whole to conclude with staggering convulsions, grinning, andc., in a manner never before publickly attempted.

The doors to be opened at eight, and the exhibition to begin precisely at nine. Particular places, for that night only, reserved for the ladies. No money to be returned, nor half price taken. Vivant Rex et Regina.

N.B. Beware of counterfeits and impostors.—The person who advertises to hang himself the same night, in opposition to Mr. Touchwood, is a taylor, who intends only to give the representation of death by dancing in a collar, an attempt infinitely inferior to Mr. T.'s original and authentic performance.

Probably camels were not seen in America before 1789. Increased interest attaches to the following advertisement from the fact that the exhibition was held near the very pump which Hawthorne commemorates in "Twice-Told Tales." This notice is taken from the "Salem Mercury," Aug. 4, 1789.

TO THE CURIOUS.

To be seen at Mr. Benjamin Daland's, near the town-pump, Salem.

TWO CAMELS,

Male and Female, imported from Arabia.

These stupenduous Animals are most deserving the attention of the curious, being the greatest natural curiosity ever exhibited to the publick on this continent. They are 19 hands high—have necks near 4 feet long—have a large bunch on their backs, and another under their breasts, in the form of a pedestal, on which they support themselves when lying down—they have 4 joints in their hind legs, and will travel 12 or 14 days without drinking, and carry a burthen of 1500 wt.—they are remarkably harmless and docile, and will lie down and rise at command.

Abraham was old and well stricken in age: And the Lord had blessed Abraham in all things. And Abraham said unto his eldest Servant of his house, that ruled over all that he had, Thou shalt go unto my Country, and to my Kindred, and take a Wife unto my Son Isaac. And the Servant took ten Camels, of the Camels of his Master, and departed; and went to Mesopotamia, unto the city Nahor. And he made his Camels to kneel down without the city, by a well of water, at the time of the evening, even the time that Women go out to draw water. Pure wisdom directed the Servant, and succeeded him in obtaining the consent of the Parents, Brethren and Kindred of Rebeccah, that she should go to the Land of Canaan, and become the Wife of Isaac. And they sent away Rebeccah, their Sister, with her Damsels and her Nurse, and Abraham's Servant, and his men, and they rode upon the Camels.—Gen. XXIV.

N.B.—The CAMELS will go from this town this evening.

In 1796 a mermaid was exhibited in Salem, and in 1800 a cassowary bird. The admission fee to the latter curiosity was for "grown persons" 12-1/2 cents, and for children 6-1/4 cents. The exact change could then be easily made, as the Spanish silver ninepences (12-1/2 cents) and fourpence halfpence (6-1/4 cents) were more common than any other silver pieces. The American dimes and half-dimes had not at that time got much into circulation in New England.

NATURAL CURIOSITY.

To be seen at Washington Hall, for this day only,

THE CASSOWARY,

A Bird, from the East Indies.

Its height is 5 feet, weighs near 100 pounds; it will eat half a peck of apples at a meal, swallow whole eggs, also stones and apples as large as eggs, and jump to a great height.—Goldsmith says, in his history of Animated Nature, it has the head of a Warrior, the eye of a Lion, the defence of a Porcupine, and the swiftness of a Courser.

It is fond of all kinds of vegetables and fruits. It will pick a pea out of a Child's hand without injury. Many that have seen it, say it is the greatest curiosity of the kind ever exhibited here. Children of seven years old can ride it.—Admittance for grown persons 9 pence—Children half price.

☞ The remarkable bird, called the CASSOWARY, now exhibiting in this town, is described by Goldsmith in his 3d volume of Animated Nature, page 39, American edition.—After describing him, the Doctor observes, that "the southern parts of the most eastern Indies seem to be its natural climate. His domain, if we may so call it, begins where that of the ostrich terminates. The latter has never been found beyond the Ganges; while the Cassowary is never seen nearer than the islands of Banda, Sumatra, Java, the Molucca islands, and the corresponding parts of the continent. Yet even here this animal seems not to have multiplied in any considerable degree, as we find one of the kings of Java making a present of one of these birds to the captain of a Dutch ship, considering it as a very great rarity."

Gazette, August 8, 1800.

The following notice, taken from the "Salem Gazette," July 13, 1790, has an interest to us from what it says of the likenesses "produced from a Spark of Electricity." It is difficult to conjecture what this means; though additional interest is derived from the fact of these likenesses having been presented by Dr. Franklin's grandson.

AMERICAN MUSEUM.

Mr. Peale, of Philadelphia, has lately received a number of donations for his Cabinet of Curiosities. Among them were

Likenesses of the King and Queen of France, executed on white satin, and each produced by a single spark of electricity.—Presented by Wm. Temple Franklin, Esq.——And

The Finger of Mr. Broliman (a provincial officer in the British service, in the war before the last) who was executed at Philadelphia for the murder of a Mr. Scull. This unfortunate gentleman, soured by some disgust, became weary of life. In this temper of mind, he one morning rose earlier than usual, and walked out upon the common of the city, with his fusee in hand, determined to shoot the first person he should meet. The first person he saw was a very pretty young girl, whose beauty disarmed him. The next presented was the late Dr. Cadwallader—The Doctor, bowing politely to Mr. Broliman (who, though unknown to him, had the garb and appearance of a gentleman) accosted him with "Good morning, Sir! What sport?" The Officer answered the Doctor very civilly; and was so struck with his gentlemanly manner and pleasing address, that he forebore to execute his desperate resolution: Impelled, however, by the same gloominess of disposition which actuated him when he first set out, he repaired to the Centre house, where some gentlemen were engaged at billiards—The tack of one of the players happening to strike his hat, the wretched man, eager for an opportunity of accomplishing his desire to leave the world, instantly shot Mr. Scull, one of the company, who died of the wound.

This little story affords a striking proof, that amiableness and politeness of manners are not only pleasing, but useful, in our commerce with the world.

Salem always was famous for its collections of natural and historical curiosities, and many of its houses are now well stocked with such things. Among these collections we may mention Mr. Geo. R. Curwen's antique family portraits, china, clothing, and furniture; Mr. M.A. Stickney's rare coins, old paper money, and books, autographs, etc.; Mr. H.F. Waters's rare ancient furniture (Mr. Waters is now in London, engaged in historical research in reference to American families); Mr. John Robinson's remarkable collection of Chinese coins, and scarce views of old houses of Salem; Mr. T.F. Hunt's valuable collection of Chinese books and pictures; Rev. Dr. Bolles's fine collection of works on London; Rev. B.F. McDaniel's collection of engravings, etc.; Mr. N.J. Holden's and Mr. F.P. Richardson's collections of illustrated books, autographs, etc.; besides numerous minor collections. It is not too much to say that Professor E.S. Morse's collection of Japanese pottery is certainly not surpassed in the world; the South Kensington collection in London, which is the best in Europe, does not approach it in size or importance. One of the best museums of our country was started in Salem in the latter part of the last century, and that collection is now, as is well known, in charge of the Peabody Academy of Science. Its objects of natural history have in recent years been carefully classified and arranged under the direction of Dr. Henry Wheatland, Professors Morse, Putnam, Packard, and Robinson; and its cabinets, together with those of the Essex Institute, now contain probably more unique and valuable specimens than are to be found elsewhere in this country.

The "silhouette," or cheap portrait cut in black paper, was much in vogue in New England some seventy or eighty years ago. The process was named from M. Silhouette, an honest French minister who about 1759 was noted for his advocacy of economy in everything relating to the public welfare. He received a great deal of ridicule, and hence all inexpensive things were said to be à la Silhouette. At the rooms of the Essex Institute, and in many houses in Salem, there are numerous silhouettes of former citizens of the place. Those who remember the originals consider the likenesses often very striking.

CORRECT PROFILE LIKENESSES.

MOSES CHAPMAN

Informs the Ladies and Gentlemen of Salem that he has taken a shop next to Mr. Morgan's, in North street, Salem, where he will take PROFILES in the newest and most elegant style: two of one person for 25 cents, or if desired, will paint and shade them for 75 cents.

☞ Frames, of different kinds and prices, for the Profiles may be had at the above place.

Salem, January 23, 1808.

Salem Register.

MR. BROWN

Respectfully informs the Public that having met with so extensive encouragement, he is induced to continue to cut and frame Profiles at Morse's Inn, opposite Boylston Market. Price for cutting 12-1/2 cents.

N.B. His customers are requested to apply in the morning, noon or evening, on account of his absence at other times.

Oct. 15.

N.E. Palladium, 1819.

In September, 1808, we have a notice of a circus, in which the horsemanship, according to the representations, must have equalled that of Barnum's people. It is not common to find much editorial comment in the papers of the time on such exhibitions, from which we judge that they were not considered first-class entertainments, and were not as much patronized by the clergy as at the present day.

AT THE

CIRCUS

IN BROAD-STREET, SALEM,

WILL BE EXHIBITED,

This Evening,

(If the weather permit; if not, the first fair evening)

A GRAND SCENE OF

Horsemanship,

Consisting of a number of HORNPIPES, danced by the Company on different Horses, while in full speed.

Mr. CRANDEL Dances the Hornpipe and Jumps the Whip.

Mr. FRANKLIN Dances the Hornpipe; Rides with his Toe in his Mouth; he also Leaps from the Ground to his Horse in various ways.

Mr. STEWART Dances the Hornpipe; Jumps a great height from his Horse, and with surprising agility throws himself into different attitudes while his horse is in full speed.

PETER dances the Hornpipe and Jumps the Whip; also, standing erect on his toes, rides in full speed once round the Circus.

Mr. STEWART performs the picking up of four Handkerchiefs from the ground; he also stands erect on his horse, while his horse leaps a board 3 feet from the ground.

PETER, the young African, riding backwards, dances a hornpipe; changes his position in a number of extraordinary leaps; jumps out of one hoop into another; and also, with one leap, jumps twice through a hoop; in once round the Circus leaps 4 quarters; and rides two Horses, one forward of the other.

The Horse Phœnix lies down, sits up, and eats from the table with his master.

The Grand Still Vaulting, by the Company.

Many other Extraordinary Feats performed during the Exhibition.

The performance to conclude with the Brother Miller.

The Doors opened at 5 o'clock in the Evening. The Performance begins at 6.

Price, Boxes 1 Dollar, Pit 50 Cents.——Tickets to be had at the Circus and at the Salem Hotel.

Those who please to favor the performers with their presence, are requested to take Tickets before the exhibition commences.—No pains will be spared to render the Entertainment as agreeable as possible.

Sept. 27, 1808.

Monstrous Sight!

TO be seen at A. POLLARD's Tavern, Elm Street—A white Greenland Sea BEAR, which was taken at sea, weighing 1000 wt. This animal lives either in the sea or on the land. They have been seen several leagues at sea, and sometimes floating on cakes of ice.—This animal displays a great natural curiosity.—Admittance 12 1-2 cts. ... children half price.

april 28.

[Boston] Columbian Centinel, 1810.

Just before the declaration of the last war against Great Britain "Non-Intercourse Quills" were for sale. This reminds us that most young people know but little about quills of any kind, and probably not one in a hundred knows, in these days, how to make a quill pen. Quills were in pretty general use for writing until about 1835 or 1836, when steel pens took their place to some extent, although quill pens were used by many down to a comparatively recent period, and occasionally a person may now be seen using one. Steel and silver pens were made by Shakers as early as 1824, and Cushing and Appleton had steel pens as early as 1811, according to an advertisement in the "Salem Gazette."

STEEL PENS

Just received for sale by

CUSHING and APPLETON,

Oct. 6th, 1811.

NON-INTERCOURSE QUILLS.

Cushing and APPLETON have still on hand a few thousand English QUILLS, which for a short time will be sold at the present low rate, for specie, or bills of any of the banks in Essex or Boston.—— ☞ Persons in want of Quills will please to recollect, that in about two or three weeks the NON-INTERCOURSE with Great Britain takes place, which in all probability will continue during the short time that Nation may exist, at least. Such another opportunity for purchasing can therefore never occur.

Jan. 14, 1811.

J. Greenleaf sold steel pens in Boston in 1812.

Steel Pens,

A further supply of the celebrated STEEL PENS is received by J. GREENLEAF, No. 49, Cornhill.

march 11 [1812].

SUPERIOR DESK KNIVES,

Manufactured in Paris of Damascus Steel and warranted.

Also—an assortment of Steel and Silver Pens, from the Shaker Village. For sale by

JOHN M. IVES,

Dec. 11 [1824].

Essex street.

Many young people do not know that in old times blotting-paper of the kind now in use had not been introduced. Black sand was used altogether for drying the ink on freshly written letters or ordinary writing, except in books, when the writers either waited for the ink to dry, or made China paper, taken from the inside of tea-chests, a blotter. Black sand was in general use until within thirty years or thereabouts. We have seen the sand adhering to writing which had been done more than a century. No writing-desk was complete without a sand-box.

BLACK SAND,

Which is so useful to all who have any thing to do with penmanship—for sale, at No. 34, opposite the Treasurer's-Office, in Marlborough-Street.

☞ BOOKS and STATIONARY, as usual.

Boston, May 29, 1790.

Columbian Centinel.

Country Traders,

Who are in search of penny-worths, are invited to the STORE of

John and Tho's Amory and Co.

No. 41, Marlborough-Street.

Columbian Centinel, 1790.

☞ IF the Small Pox should be allowed to spread in this town [Boston], the Editor assures his country customers that every precaution in his power shall be taken, that no part of his papers shall convey the infection into the country.—But it is his belief that it will not be permitted to spread—and his wishes accord with his belief, having never had the infection. Should he be necessitated to innoculate, he shall withdraw himself from his office and leave the business in the care of a person who will use every caution necessary for the purpose.

Columbian Centinel, Aug. 29, 1792.

Whereas a Person who

called himself by the Name of Charles Brown, did on the 29th of June last, hire a Chaise of Israel Davis, of Danvers, to go to Boston; since which the said Chaise has not been returned: This is to give Notice to any one who will discover the said Brown or Chaise, and leave Word with the Printers hereof, a Reward of Ten Dollars for each, will be given by

Israel Davis.

The said Brown is of a middling Stature, thin, looked sickly and very poor, as if he had had the yellow Fever: He is about 30 Years of Age; wears short black Hair, tied with a black Ribbon; has a blue German Serge Surtout Coat, faced with blue Calamancoe, yellow Buttons; a whitish Coat and Breeches; blue Sattin Jacket, with a narrow scollop'd Silver Lace: He has also a yellowish Thicksett Coat, blue Plush Waistcoat, yellow Leather Breeches, a laced Hat, and ruffled Shirts; appears and pretends to be a Gentleman, and has a Person with him as a Waiter, who calls himself Capt Stutson.

The Chaise has standing Posts with a Canvass Top, the Lining is cloth coloured Broad-Cloth; the back is warped by the Sun and cracked; the Leather at the Bottom of the Floor old; large Brass Nails on the Foot Board; the Door of the Box is pricked with Awl-Holes; one of the Staples thro' which the Reins go on the Saddle is loose; The off-wheel has two Gripes thereon.

Danvers, July 10, 1762.

Boston Gazette.

THIS DAY PUBLISHED,

And to be Sold at the New Printing Office in Cornhill (Price four Coppers), THE Two Mothers; or The History of Antigone and Phronissa; Shewing how Antigone laughed at her good old Grandmother, and married her Daughters, before Sixteen, to a laced Coat and a fashionable Wig,——and how the wiser Phronissa instructed her Daughters in Reading, Dressing, Singing, Dancing, Visiting, andc. in order to make them happy and useful in the rising Age.

Boston Gazette, Oct. 8, 1759.

New Establishment.

The Subscriber, desirous of doing all in his power whereby he can serve the public, and at the same time benefit himself, is induced to give this public notice, that he has removed to the New Assembly House, Chestnut Street, where he proposes opening a

RESTORATOR,

for the accommodation of all who may honor him with their calls. Ample arrangements have been made and he flatters himself that superior cooking and good attendance will secure the patronage of a liberal public.

☞ SOUP will be served up at 11 a.m. on Mondays, Tuesdays, Thursdays and Fridays during the winter.

All kinds of Cakes, Wafers, French Rolls, andc. furnished at the shortest notice.

JOHN REMOND.

TURTLE SOUP.

Two GREEN TURTLES will be served up, as above, This Day, at 11 and 1 o'clock. Families supplied by immediate application.

Salem, Oct. 24 [1815].

Salem Gazette.

Speaking Figure.

The Proprietor respectfully informs the publick that his exhibition will remain in Boston until sold or removed to New-York. More fully to gratify the curiosity of the publick, the Speaking Figure is moved to a part of the room which intirely removes the suspicion of any one being concealed in the chimney.—Those who wish to see this most pleasing phenomenon of art will please to call soon, as this will positively be the last day.

Those who have viewed the exhibition in its former situation will be charged half price for re-admission—those who have not, are admitted at 1s6. each, from 3 o'clock in the afternoon until 9 in the evening, by the Publick's most obedient,

SAMUEL PRINCE.

Boston, Oct. 16, 1790.

Columbian Centinel.

We frequently find in old Boston papers advertisements of rare beasts to be exhibited,—in December, 1800, a "Beautiful Moose," and in August, 1801, a "Beautiful Lion."

TO THE CURIOUS.

A beautiful African LION,

To be seen every day in the week (Sundays excepted) in Brattle-street, next to Major King's, near the Market, where a very convenient situation is provided for those Ladies and Gentlemen who may please to favor the proprietor with their presence.

This noble Animal is between three and four feet high, measures eight feet from nostrils to tail, and a beautiful dun colour; 11 years old, and weighs near 500 wt.—His legs and tail are as thick as those of a common size ox. He was caught in the woods of Goree, in Africa, when a whelp; and brought from thence to New-York. Great attention has been paid in providing a strong substantial Cage, and to have the Lion under very good command. The person who has the care of him can comb his mane, make him lie down and get up at any time; and it is said by those who have seen Lions in the Tower of London, and many parts, that he is really worth the contemplation of the curious.

☞ Admittance 25 Cents.—Children half price.

Aug. 13 [1801].

Boston Gazette.

A Beautiful MOOSE.

The curious in Natural History are invited to Major King's Tavern, where is to be seen a fine young MOOSE of sixteen hands in height, and well proportioned. The properties of this fleet and tractable Animal are such as will give pleasure and satisfaction to every beholder.

Price of admittance, Nine Pence.

Dec. 9, 1800.

Massachusetts Mercury.

We have before noticed the tastes of the people formerly for wax-work. In 1805 there was another curious collection in Salem.

WAX-WORK.

STREET and GROSE respectfully acquaint the Ladies and Gentlemen of Salem that there is now exhibiting at Washington Hall a new and elegant collection of well executed WAX FIGURES, (large as life,) consisting of the following characters, viz.

A striking representation of the late unfortunate

DUEL between

General Hamilton, and

Colonel Burr.

In this interesting scene the General is represented

as supported by his Second, after receiving the

fatal wound, while the Second of Colonel

Burr urges him to retire from the field.

An excellent likeness of the

Marquis De La Fayette.

The Austere Father

Frowning upon his DAUGHTER, finding her

with her Gallant.

The handsome Coquette.

PROSPERO and CALABAN, a scene from the Tempest.

OTHELLO and DESDEMONA: this scene is taken from Shakespeare's celebrated play of the Moor of Venice. Othello is represented as meditating on the murder of his amiable and beautiful wife. The curtains that surround the bed of Desdemona are superb, and formerly encircled that of the Queen of France. The scene of Othello is an object of admiration.

The SALEM BEAUTY.

The FEMALE ECONOMIST, a Lady giving instructions to her Daughter.

TIANA, Prince of Atooi.

CALICUM, a Chief of Nookta Sound.

WYNEE, a native of Owyhee.

LIBERTY and JUSTICE supporting a portrait of Gen. WASHINGTON.

A BUST of General BONAPARTE, in Plaster of Paris, said to be a correct likeness.

A GLASS SHIP.

A Likeness of

A Child

Now living in Newhaven, which at its birth weighed only two pounds and fourteen ounces.

The Grecian Daughter,

Nourishing her Father in prison.

A striking likeness of

Jason Fairbanks,

Who was executed at Dedham, and of the beautiful

Eliza Fales:

He is dressed in the same Clothes that he wore at the time of his trial.

Also—Sundry other interesting Figures.

Music on the Organ.

The Exhibition will be open from nine o'clock in the morning until nine in the evening, (Saturday evening and Sunday excepted,) and will be removed from this town shortly.

Admittance 25 Cents—Children half price.

☞ No person will be allowed to touch any of the figures above mentioned.

Salem, June 14.

Our grandfathers and grandmothers sometimes had dealings with large sums of money.

To the Curious

TO be seen at Jeremiah Bulfinch's, near the Mill-Bridge, a live

HOG,

That is thought to be the biggest ever raised in this Country, weighing upwards of 1000 weight. The price for viewing of said quadruped is 4 pence.

March 2 [1791].

Herald of Freedom.
To Widow Keziah Bartlett.
Your Tax for 1810, committed to J. Newell
for Collection, is d.c.
State Tax 0 3
County and Town 0 14

_____

$0 17
JOSEPH NEWELL.
Feb. 24, 1813.
Collector of Needham.
Boston Patriot.
To Widow Keziah Bartlett.
Your Tax for 1811, committed to Jesse Daniell for Collection, is
d.c.
State Tax— 0 3
County and Town— 0 13

_____

$0.16
JESSE DANIELL,
Feb. 24, 1813.
Collector of Needham.
Boston Patriot.
NOTICE.
The Annual Meeting of the Boston Cent Society will be holden at the
House of Mrs. MARGARET PHILLIPS, Walnut street, on Tuesday, April
8th, at 11 o'clock A.M. The subscribers are requested to attend.
Per Order
April 5.
Columbian Centinel, 1817.
ONE MILL REWARD.
Ran away from the subscriber, an indented Apprentice, of the name of
JAMES BAILS. All persons are hereby forbidden to trust or harbor him on
my account. (Signed)
THOMAS CAINES.
South-Boston, August 8, 1817.
Columbian Centinel.
The "Jews-Harp Club" indicates the state of music in Salem in 1815.
Jews-Harp Club.
The first meeting of this Society will be holden at the Essex Coffee House,
This Evening at 8 o'clock, for the purpose of electing Officers and
organizing the Society.
April 25, 1815.

In 1814 the Essex Coffee House in Salem, formerly the residence of the Hon. William Gray (Lieutenant-Governor of Massachusetts), was opened by Prince Stetson, as the following advertisements show.

ESSEX COFFEE-HOUSE.

Prince STETSON informs the public that he has closed the doors of the Salem Hotel and taken that spacious and elegant brick house, (the late mansion of the Hon. Wm. Gray,) in Essex-Street, a few rods west of the Sun Tavern, now known by the name of the ESSEX COFFEE-HOUSE; where he will be happy to accommodate Travellers, Parties, Fire Clubs, and all other guests who may honor him with their company.

He rests his claims for patronage on a Larder well supplied with the choicest viands which the markets afford—a cellar stocked with the best Wines and other Liquors which can be procured—and the assiduous attention of civil and capable Servants, together with his own personal exertions to give every satisfaction to his guests. [6w]

Salem, July 4, 1814.

THE CLOSED DOOR—OPEN.

That Mr. Stetson, on leaving the SALEM HOTEL, shut the door after him, is probable enough: it is what is expected of every well-bred man on leaving any house; but

GRAY and CARTER

beg leave to inform the public that the door is now opened again, and though the Hotel is not so spacious as the Prince-ly Mansion of their neighbour, yet being an old and well accustomed Stand, they flatter themselves that those gentlemen who have long frequented it, will not discontinue their custom, as no pains will be spared to accommodate Parties—Fire Clubs—steady Boarders, and all who may honor the house with their company. ☞ Particular attention will be paid to Gentlemen's Horses and Carriages.

July 13 [1814].

We seldom hear nowadays of so scandalous an act as is here set forth; although there was a time in England when it was proved that murders were committed solely for the purpose of selling the bodies of the victims to surgeons for dissection.

500 Dollars Reward.

Most daring and sacrilegious Robbery.

Stolen, from the grave yard in Chebacco Parish in Ipswich, the bodies of eight persons, seven of whom were interred since the 13th of October last; the other, a coloured man, about six years ago. As without doubt they have all, ere this time, passed under the dissecting knife of the anatomist, either of the rude novice in the art or of the skilful professor, little hope is entertained of recovering any relict of them for the consolation of the deeply afflicted friends. But whoever will give any information of this atrocious villainy, so as to detect and bring to justice, either the traders in this abominable traffic, or their inhuman employers, shall receive the above reward; and the thanks of an afflicted and distressed people.

WILLIAM ANDREWS jun.

THOMAS CHOATE

NATHAN BURNHAM

Ipswich, Chebacco Parish, } Committee.

April 25th, 1818.

Business in "Knocker's Hole" must have been brisker in 1811 than it has been of late years. Old Salem people will remember "Roast Meat Hill."

Distress in the Baking Business!

Cash spoiling for want of good labor, as my brethren have distressed me so by giving all the workmen in this town steady employ, so that I have not bread to oblige my good customers in season. To relieve myself, I offer to six Journeymen Bakers of other towns, who can recommend themselves by good and quick dispatch in that line of business, $15 per month for this season.——Wanted, two LABORERS about the yard, two months or more; 8 in all more than my present number may have good employ by calling on

SAMUEL BATHRICK,

Baker, Mill-street, Salem, Massachusetts, easily found by inquiry.

July 12 [1811].

Sport in 1821.

TO SPORTSMEN.

The Subscriber, intending to give a grand treat to Sportsmen and Sharp Shooters, purposes to set up a number of fine TURKEYS to be fired at on FRIDAY, the 7th day of December next, and invites all who are disposed for this purpose to attend.

Good accommodations will be found at his house.

JOHN T. DODGE, jr.

Wenham, Nov. 23, 1821.

Sharp Shooting.

THOMAS D. POUSLAND informs his friends and the friends of Sport that he will, on FRIDAY, the 7th day of December next, set up for SHOOTING a number of

Fine Fat TURKEYS,

and invites all the gunners and others, who would wish to recreate themselves, to call on the day after Thanksgiving at the Old Baker's Tavern, Upper Parish, Beverly, where every accommodation can be afforded.

Nov. 23.

Salem Gazette.

What was expected of a governess in 1817.

WANTED.

Wanted, an intelligent and well informed LADY, above or about forty years of age, as a governess, capable of instructing four young Children of her own sex in all the early branches, to reside in the family of their father, a gentleman of high respectability in every sense of the word, and of considerable fortune and estate, upon which he dwells, in the vicinity of Winchester, Frederick County, Virginia. It will be expected that she understands and will undertake at same time the management and direction of the household and family concerns. For further information, application may be made to the subscriber, now residing for a short time at the house of Mr. Thomas Lewis, Cambridge-street, Boston, near Mr. Lowell's Meeting-house.

august 13.   ep3t   JOHN HOLKER.

Columbian Centinel.

BULL-FIGHT IN NEW ENGLAND!

Many persons have supposed that bull-fights were never to be seen except in Spain; but it appears that in June, 1809, according to an advertisement in the "Essex Register," there was to be a bull-fight on the Salem turnpike, near the "Half-way House" (to Boston). As there were no reporters in those days, we are unable to give an account of the exhibition.

Sportsmen, Attend!

The gentlemen SPORTSMEN of this town and its vicinity are informed that a Grand Combat will take place between the URUS, ZEBU, and Spanish BULL, on the 4th of July, if fair weather, if not, the next fair day, at the Half-way House on the Salem Turnpike. There will also be exposed at the Circus, other Animals, which, for courage, strength and sagacity are inferior to none. No danger need be apprehended during the performance, as the Circus is very convenient.

Doors opened at 3, performance to begin at 4. Tickets 50 cents.

After the performance there will be a grand FOX CHASE on the Marshes near the Circus, to start precisely at 6 o'clock.

General Fencing Exhibition

Messrs. TROMELLE and GIRARD, Fencing-Masters of the Military School of Col. de la Croix, respectfully inform the Gentlemen of Salem and its vicinity that they propose a

FENCING EXHIBITION,

at which several amateurs will be present, and during which they will play the Small-Sword, Cut-and-Thrust, Broad-Sword, and Cudgel or Cane Fighting; to close with a Duel between Messrs. T. and G., who will at first fight with Sabres, and afterwards with Small-Swords, until one of the parties falls weltering in blood.

The Exhibition will be on FRIDAY, the 30th inst., at 7 o'clock P.M., at the Military School, Washington Hall, Court street.

Terms of admission, One Dollar.

Tickets to be had at Mr. Crombie's Salem Hotel, and at Mr. Tucker's Sun-Tavern.

June 23.

Essex Register.

Something like the stylographic pen was advertised in 1825 in Salem.

The self-supplying

Pocket Writing Instrument,

OR

Scheffer's Patent Penograph.

The merit of this Instrument is that it contains Ink, and supplies itself as required, by which means the writer is enabled to use it for 10 or 12 hours with the same ease as with a pencil, without the aid of an Inkstand; and is manufactured in Gold or Silver, either with or without a pencil case, and so constructed that either a Metallic or Quill Nib may be applied. For sale by June 24 [1825].

J.R. BUFFUM.

A "caravan" of 1824.

A CARAVAN OF

LIVING ANIMALS

Is now exhibiting at the Essex Coffee House, in this town.

Among the Animals are the following:—

The African Lion.

The beautiful spotted Lama, from the Coast of Peru.

The Mammoth Ox, 6 years old, 18 hands high, 16 feet in length, and raised in Chenango county, State of New York. He is well worthy the attention of the public.

The Dwarf Cow, 7 years old, 2 feet 4 inches in height, and is handsomely proportioned. This most extraordinary and wonderful production of nature has been visited by a large number of persons, in different cities, and is pronounced a complete model in miniature of her kind; she is so short that she can pass under the belly of the large Ox.

The Heifer, 3 years old, having 6 legs, and is very active.

Two large Bears, very tractable and docile.

Dandy Jack.

Saucy Jack.

The Great Ribbed Nose Baboon.

The beautiful Deer, 2 years old.

The Ichneumon, an animal famous for destroying reptiles' eggs, and is worshipped by the Egyptians.

Also, a variety of other Animals, Birds, andc.

☞ Admittance 12 1-2 cents; Children under 12 years of age, half price. Open from 9 A.M. till 9 P.M., Saturday evenings excepted. The room is conveniently fitted, so that Ladies and Gentlemen can view the animals with perfect safety.

This Exhibition is attended with good Music on different instruments. Also, Music on the Leaf. The sounds produced by the Leaf are admired by the lovers of Music.

Jan. 30.

Salem Gazette.

It may be interesting to some of our readers to see what piano music was popular in 1827-1829.

Elias Hook, the celebrated organ-builder, of the firm of E. and G.G. Hook and Hastings, was a native of Salem and kept a music-store there, moving to Boston about 1830.

NEW

Piano Forte Music.

Just published, and for sale by ELIAS HOOK,

The Maltese Boat Song; Polly Hopkins and Tommy Tompkins; The Soldier's last Sigh; 'Tis sweet to take the bonnie Lake; When I left thy shores, O Naxos; The merry Flageolet; When young men come a sighing; Comin' thro' the Rye; Love was once a little Boy; I've been Roaming; My Heart and Lute; Draw the Sword, Scotland; Adventures of Paul Pry; I have Fruit and I have Flowers; The Washing Day; The Light Guitar, and Answer; Long Summers have smiled—andc. andc. [1827].

New Piano Music.

Yon ROSE TREE. The Rock of our Salvation. Thou art my only Love. The days of good Queen Bess. Gipsey Rondo. Oh, 'tis Love. As the evening Appearing. The cup of Love. The Bells of St. Andrew's Tower. By murmuring brook. The Banner of Battle. A fragrant Rose there grew. My country no more. To live and Love. My own native Isle. Mild is thine eye of blue, sweet maid. Mary of the Ferry. Look you now. Love thee, yes, too fondly, truly. Lovely Mary. Love in the Barn. Bolivar's Peruvian Battle Song. There is a Love. The Glasses sparkle on the Board. St. Patrick was a Gentleman. The winter it is past. With Instructions—for the Piano andc. just received by

March 29 [1829].

J.M. IVES.

In February, 1829, Mr. Nazro, of the Roundhill School (Northampton?), made the following singular challenge to Edwin Forrest, the tragedian. We do not know whether or not it was accepted.

The Boston Evening Bulletin of Wednesday last contains the following:—

"A Card. If Mr. Edwin Forrest, the Tragedian, thinks that more effect can be produced by reading Tragedy than can be by reading from Scripture, Mr. Nazro, Instructor of Elocution, from Roundhill School, would deny it fully, and offers to meet him, Mr. Forrest, in any town in the United States, and read from Scripture, and Mr. Forrest shall read from Tragedy.

Boston, 25th Feb., 1829."

The "draisena" was the forerunner of the velocipede and bicycle.

THE DRAISENA.

Ambrose SALISBURY, Wheelwright and Chaise-Maker, first introduced into this town [Boston] Machines similar to the one described below, and of which the plate will convey some idea; he has manufactured two, which may be examined at his Shop in Water-street, where the manner of using them will be explained. It is called Draisena, from the name of the Inventor. May 7.

N.E. Palladium, 1819.

Advertisements of John Remond, for many years well known in Salem as a caterer. He used to advertise very freely. He was the father of Charles Lenox Remond, the famous colored lecturer.

Salem,

SATURDAY, NOVEMBER 11, 1820.

TURTLE SOUP

The subscriber will issue from his

house in Chesnut-street, on Tuesday and Wednesday next, at from 12 to 1 o'clock, SOUP made from a superior fat Turtle, weighing over 200 wt.

His old customers and the public will be supplied as usual at 50 cts per quart.

J. REMOND.

NOTICE.

The subscriber informs his customers that notwithstanding he has publicly discontinued the sale of OYSTERS, in consequence of their being in an unhealthy state during the months of July and August, still he is ready to supply them as usual, if called upon; he would observe, however, that he cannot hold himself responsible for the injurious effects they may produce on the system when eaten at this season of the year.

JOHN REMOND.

July 16 [1831].

HAMILTON HALL,

CHESTNUT STREET.

This Establishment having been purchased by a New Company, and undergone repairs, the interior of the same is so far completed that the subscriber is ready for the reception of Genteel Parties. The repairs and improvements already made; the furnace which heats the entire Dancing portion of the building,—entries, Supper Hall, etc.; the improved Chandelier, new Sofas, Ladies' drawing-room new carpeted and furnished in a comfortable manner; a reduction of former price of Hall; strict adherence to a uniform price of Help, and every care taken to select and furnish the most careful and obliging attendants, with the enchanting music of the Salem Quadrille Band, cannot fail to secure the patronage of a generous public. Did I say above, "enchanting music"? Yes. Without the fear of contradiction, during thirty years and upwards that it has been my privilege to conduct the affairs of Hamilton Hall, I have never heard from five instruments richer music sent forth than I did on the evening of the 27th November, ultimo.—There is one fact that should be known, and which is acknowledged by all who have performed there, that five pieces of music are better in Hamilton Hall than seven in any other Hall in the city.

As respects the subscriber, who is still to conduct the affairs of the establishment, suffice it to say that those who have had the pleasure, for a long series of years, to participate in such matters, are the best judges of the style, comfort, etc.

REMOND.

N.B. With the extensive cooking apparatus and other advantages of the premises, Families who do not wish to disarrange their houses, or single gentlemen who are not at House-keeping, wishing to entertain their friends, can be accommodated at reasonable prices, and everything conducted in true family style.

J.R.

Salem, Dec. 16 [1844].